GOLF
AND
MURPHY'S
LAW

Mervyn J. Huston

Illustrated by
Graham Pilsworth

Hurtig Publishers
Edmonton

Hurtig Publishers Ltd.
10560—105 Street
Edmonton, Alberta

Canadian Cataloguing in Publication Data

Huston, Mervyn J., 1912–
  Golf and Murphy's Law

  ISBN 0-88830-208-8

  1. Golf—Anecdotes, facetiae, satire, etc.
2. Murphy's law.   I. Pilsworth, Graham, 1944-
II. Title.

GV967.H87   796.352'02'07   C81-091245-7

Printed and bound in Canada
by T. H. Best Printing Company Ltd.

○○○

Contents

○○○

This book is dedicated
to my golfing pals at Mililani...

MJH

...and to Jamie and Nicholas.

GP

I would like to acknowledge
the remarkable ability of Stephanie Ussyk
to type the manuscript from my
all-but-indecipherable handwriting.

MJH

Thank you very much Richard Whyte
for the collage assistance.

GP

Introduction

Murphy's Law: *if anything can go wrong, it will,* has become part of contemporary folklore. This great philosophical truth has been wholeheartedly accepted by the denizens of our complex society as an explanation for things going awry. Furthermore, the popularity of the precept rests in large part upon the fact that it provides an escape from responsibility; once Murphy has been invoked, any problem is understandable. Nobody wants to take the blame for anything, so buck-passing is standard procedure and a well-refined art. In large organizations such as governments, the buck can be passed in circles until it disappears. Another fate for the buck is that it may eventually get passed high enough in a hierarchy to reach a person who is too important to bother with it. However, when the buck is passed downwards, as usually happens, this happy resolution does not take place. When all else fails, the buck stops with Murphy. In entrepreneurial activities, such as golf, where there is no one to blame but yourself or Murphy, Murphy gets the nod. What a useful fellow.

Manifestations of Murphy's Law are to be found in all human endeavour, from a slice of bread falling butter side down on the rug, to the malfunctioning of missiles. It is no wonder that there has been such universal adoption of the now famous apophthegm which bears Murphy's name.

Nobody knows who the great Murphy was. Some nominations have been put forward but none of these are persuasive and they smack of efforts to cash in retroactively on a good thing. No, Murphy remains anonymous and he must rank as one of the great unidentified heroes of all time, along with whoever discovered the wheel and the genius who first proposed income taxes. Even if it were known who Murphy was, his identity would have been submerged in the importance of his discovery, as happened to other great benefactors of mankind such as Mr. Crapper, Mrs. Bloomer, Herr Ohm, the Earl of Sandwich, and Mr. Titslinger.

It is surprising, as with all great discoveries, that the law of mischance as promulgated by Murphy was not enunciated earlier. Perhaps it was but got mislaid because something went wrong—which figures. This sort of philosophical revelation was one of the great strengths of the Greek sages, but it must be conceded that the name Murphy scarcely has a Hellenistic sound to it—unless he was originally Murpholopolos. However, all important advances of knowledge are based upon information which accumulates from a variety of sources but remains stagnant until it is examined by the mind of a genius. He puts the evidence together, cries "aha" or "eureka," and a great truth bursts upon the world. Immediately thereafter, others emerge to claim they thought of it first—usually a Russian (anyone for Murphovich?). But such claims are irrelevant. The person who deserves to be acclaimed is the one who first made the information known to the world. So let us give full credit to Murphy—whoever he was.

Basic Principles

○○○

Murphy's Law has been elaborated, refined and applied in a variety of ways. Strangely, until now there has been no important attempt to analyze the awesome significance of the precept in the game of golf. It is surprising that this hiatus in Murphology exists, because in no other field are the manifestations of Murphy's Law more evident than in this noble sport. I have a theory that Murphy arrived at his great discovery because he was a golfer and that the wider application to other fields came later. Newton was hit on the head by an apple, which led him to discover one of the great laws of physics; Murphy was probably hit on the head by a golf ball.

Murphy's Law Applied to Golf would read: *If anything can go wrong with a golf shot, it will.* I shall present evidence in support of this thesis and discuss the significance of my findings to the game. These data will be epitomized in supplementary, ancillary and spin-off laws, rules and maxims ("Huston's Laws of Perverse Golf"). I shall also present certain precepts relating to the human comedy in a golfing environment, although not directly applicable to the game itself.

I shall assume that you know something about the game of golf—otherwise you wouldn't be reading this book. However, in case you are not too familiar with the Royal and Ancient sport, I should explain that the objective of golf is to knock a ball into a specified hole in the ground from a specified distance, with the least number of blows—like some other things in life, easy in conception but difficult in delivery.

I have chosen to write from the point of view of a duffer for the very good reason that I have no alternative. However, this is fortuitous for a number of reasons. The term "duffer" is a relative thing; to a pro anyone with a handicap over five is a duffer, but that's not what I have in mind. I shall leave the limits of dufferdom somewhat vague so that the reader can relate to the term according to his or her own level of expertise. However, the vast majority of golfers fall into the category of duffer by any criterion, so I am assured that my approach will appeal to the largest number of empathetic ears. Furthermore, the manifestations of Murphy's Law are more apt to appear in this group if for no other reason than that they take more strokes. No doubt the pros feel that they are haunted by a malefic Murphy too, but that's their business and I shall ignore them.

Golf is a series of shots, each of which presents its unique problems. In any round, let us assume a hundred blows for ease of calculation and because that figure fits the greatest number of golfers. In every shot there are an infinite number of ways for things to go awry. Therefore, no two manifestations of Murphy's Law are identical, unless the ball is missed completely, and even then it will be missed in different ways and for different reasons. Very few golf shots are an all-or-nothing proposition—except on water holes. It must be realized that the result of any shot has an effect, for good or ill, upon subsequent shots. An extreme example of this sequence is the Domino Theory of Escalating Disasters (see later).

If we compare the size of a golf ball with the area fore and aft (rebounds, you know) waiting to receive the ball, we are brought to the **First Law of Probability** which reads: *wherever a golf ball is meant to go, there is no probability that it will go there.* When the shot is made by a duffer with a high potential for aberration, a larger number of possibilities arises as to the ultimate resting place of the ball. Thus we meet the **Duffer's Corollary to the First Law of Probability**, which states: *the higher the handicap, the higher the negative probability of the ball going wherever it should go.* This corollary proves the

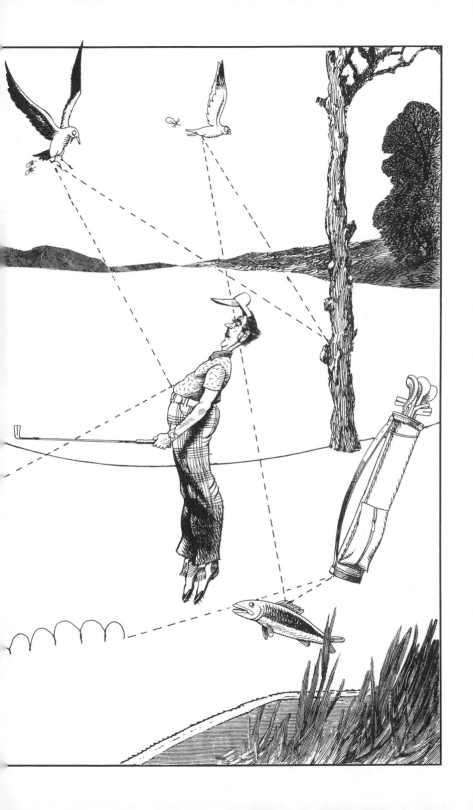

validity of the original law. The regrettable significance is that the higher the negative probability, the higher the possibility of a lousy shot.

All golfers are subject to Murphy's Basic Law, but each one is convinced that he has been particularly singled out for victimization. Cries heard on the course testify to this belief, such as: "Wouldn't you know it"; "It could only happen to me"; "It's just not my day"; "Not for me"; and "Why me?" These golfers will hold forth loud and long in the bar later as to the selective enmity of fate.

There may be validity to some of these claims. A statement made by Mrs. Murphy to a group of her cronies over a cup of tansy tea is pertinent here, and demonstrates that she had a sagacity at least equal to that of her distinguished husband. I shall take the liberty of putting her comment in the form of a law. **Mrs. Murphy's Law** states: *if there's some way to screw things up, my husband will find it.* She introduced into the Murphy equation the human element, which has considerable significance. Her observation has universal application—if you have any doubt about it, ask your spouse. Mrs. Murphy's revealing comment casts a new light on the possibly devious motivation of Murphy in formulating his famous principle. Could it be that Murphy was simply trying to obscure in generalities an intrinsic personal characteristic? Such a possibility is disquieting because it calls into question the soundness of those who have used his law over the years as an explanation for things going badly. A natural law is supposed to be impersonal and to apply to everyone equally. Maybe it doesn't. Some people are accident-prone; some may be Murphy-prone.

The incidence of things going awry varies considerably from day to day. Certainly, some days (when Murphy's star is in the ascendancy) you would have been better to have stayed in bed. The difficulty is that you don't know until afterwards which days to avoid. Some cultures use soothsayers and diviners to identify these periods in advance. (Italian golfers never play on the Ides of March.) However, such divinations lack scientific validity and are subject to the dangers of *post hoc* reasoning, so there's no value in studying the entrails of sheep or the flight of ravens to find out if you should stay away from the course on any particular day. Although outright propitiation of evil spirits has largely gone out of style, golfers are the most superstitious bunch of citizens since Stonehenge went into eclipse—horse players not excepted. Every golfer carries his good-luck charm or continues to wear the lucky hat he had on when he won the Blossom Open. **The Law of the Occult** reads: *all golfers say they are not superstitious, but subscribe to some form of sorcery, just in case.*

Murphy merely smiles.

One seeming amelioration of the baleful influence of Murphy comes under the heading of serendipity. A serendipitous shot is one that is just terrible but the results of which are just dandy.

How many times has your opponent sculled an approach shot with a pitching wedge and had the ball skitter along the ground, bang into the flag pole, then drop into the hole? I've seen a ball (not mine) in full flight across the green on its way to disaster, catch the flag fluttering in the breeze and drop into the hole. At such times some clown will come up with the old cliché, "It's not how but how many!" Much more spectacular shots are seen from time to time, such as a ball deflecting off two trees, bouncing off a bench and the ball washer, to end up on the green. However, the sad truth of fortuity in golf is found in the **Law of Serendipity**: *serendipitous shots are made more frequently by your opponents than by yourself.*

Golf is neither a game of skill nor of chance. Golf is a vicious, no-holds-barred struggle with Murphy.

The First Tee

The first tee represents the triumph of hope over experience. Forgotten are the disasters of the last game and the twelve games before that; remembered are the successes of a year ago August. The former are aberrations, the latter are expected. Today everything will fall into place and the round will be the triumph which has heretofore been elusive because of a few ridiculous intrusions by Murphy, which couldn't possibly happen again. Still, there is that niggling, frightening doubt that Murphy may again put in an appearance and screw things up.

Let us look in on the first tee on a sunny Saturday morning. There is an ambience of excitement, tension, apprehension, and, in some cases, sheer terror. What a turbulence, what a commotion! Golfers strutting about in their best bib and tucker; swinging one, two or three clubs back and forth; practice putting (the balls go into the hole as if they had eyes); checking with the starter on tee-off times; choosing partners (the usual clichés— "Give me a ball and we'll throw up." "Let's all throw up."); people without games trying to find an opening; settling the stakes ("The usual? buck, buck, buck and press when you're two down—or feel down."); haggling for strokes ("You rotten robber! Sandbagger! Hustler!"); ponderous badinage; watching for late arrivals; announcements by the starter on the P.A. system. The backstage at LaScala on opening night is halcyon by comparison.

Over this whole hurly-burly hovers the spirit of Murphy like a malign miasma. Everybody is subconsciously aware of his influence because they've been there before—and so has Murphy. Furthermore, all the laws of golfing mischance are exacerbated on the first tee, as evidenced by the **First Variation to Murphy's Law of Golf**: *the chance of things going wrong with a golf shot goes up in direct proportion to the number of people watching.*

There are a number of ways of preparing yourself for the terrors of the first tee. One way is to have a good slug of scotch. This has been tried many times but doesn't work worth a damn unless you are Scottish. The Scots do everything better with a wee dram of usquebaugh under their sporrans. But if you are not of that ilk, I advise against it. True, a snort may relax you, but judging the degree of relaxation is a dicey proposition and you might end up in a flower-bed on your back swing.

Another technique is to go to the practice fairway before teeing off. This doesn't work at all, and ignores the **First Law of Practice Fairways**: *if you have a bad session on the practice fairway you will have a lousy round.* **Second Law**: *if you have a good session, you will have a lousy round anyhow.*

The most common procedure in preparing yourself for the first tee, or for any shot for that matter, is to take practice swings—take lots of them. The **First Rule of Practice Swings** states: *no matter how many practice swings you have taken, it is a good idea to take another one, or maybe two.* On the first tee, when facing the ball, taking a large number of practice swings has the additional effect of postponing the moment of truth. However, you should be aware of the **Law of Inevitability**: *the longer you postpone the inevitable, the more inevitable it becomes.* Eventually, you're going to have to take your courage in your hands and hit the goddamned thing.

The first rule of practice swings is the abundant swing procedure followed by most golfers. However, this rule runs smack dab into the **Second Rule of Practice Swings**: *the more practice swings a golfer takes, the worse the real shot.*

The paradox of two golf rules conflicting is not unusual, and is explained by the source of the rules, *i.e.*, whether they are intrinsically, or extrinsically generated. What golfers actually do arises from intrinsic compulsions; this produces a rule of practice. An examination of the effect of that rule on performance will disclose whether or not the result is advantageous or otherwise. (Your author is part Irish and frequently gets entangled in the convolutions of his own logic. But we'll work it out.) If the application of the rule is supportive of the desired result, then no conflict arises; but if the practice proves to be inimical, then an extrinsic rule is promulgated which is contrary to the intrinsic rule. Golfers will continue to use the intrinsic rule because its genesis is compulsive. This paradox explains why golfers continue to do many things which don't work. The question arises: does a large number of practice swings produce a bad shot or do bad golfers take more practice swings? In other words, is the progression causal or casual? The answer is to be found in the **Law of Cause and Effect in Golf**, which reads: *in golf, the law of cause and effect does not apply.*

On the first tee you see practice swingers all over the place—off to the side, behind trees, in the parking lot, and, finally, on the tee head. What things of beauty! How smooth, how co-ordinated, how powerful. Slow back-swing, and good follow-through, effective transfer of weight. Great! Try it slow-motion: examine the club at the top of the back-swing; hold the follow-through for analysis of hands, elbows and stomach; gaze far down the fairway where the ball is going to go. Some of these practice swingers look as if they were rehearsing for Swan Lake and should be wearing leotards with the padded jockstraps affected by male ballet dancers. All in vain. Any comparison between the smooth swing and the spastic lurch when the ball is in front of them is coincidental. The **Third Rule of Practice Swings** states: *the smoother the practice swing, the jerkier the real thing.*

At six-minute intervals the Starter announces the names of the next foursome to tee off. The hopefuls sort themselves out and make their way to the tee, followed by jocular and ribald comment from the bystanders. The partnerships, the stakes and the order of hitting have been previously determined by traditional methods. The player chosen to hit first goes to the tee, sets his ball up, and begins his preliminary exercises.

Every golfer has his own set of nervous twitches and contortions to go through in preparation for the ultimate moment. Some of these rituals are quite elaborate and follow a rigid pattern. If any factor interrupts one of these countdowns to blast-off, the golfer has to start the series all over again. Each golfer is convinced that every other golfer's manoeuvres are ridiculous, counter-productive and overly long. This is true. But every golfer thinks his own preliminaries are short, efficient and productive. This is not true. The **Rule of Preliminaries** states: *the longer the preliminaries, the worse the shot.*

When the golfer appears to ready to hit the ball, the Starter hollers, "Man on the tee," and the noise and movement around the tee stop abruptly. A cathedral-like hush falls upon the group—practice swingers stop swinging, putters stop putting, conversations cease in mid-sentence, bees stop buzzing, birds cease their twittering, and no one moves a muscle. If anyone coughs he gets a dirty look. (Pity poor Elmer Throgmorton who inevitably reacted to the tension of the first tee by getting hiccups. He was banished from the club and took up lawn bowling.) This hush focuses all attention on the hapless bastard on the tee—attention he would much prefer be directed elsewhere. When he has hit the ball, the movement and babble renew, like turning on a tap. Depending on the quality of the shot, you hear an envious "Great shot," or an insincere "Tough luck," or a lukewarm "That'll play." The performer picks up his tee and, if Murphy defeated, swaggers off with a moue of false modesty, saying "Only got part of the ball"; or, if Murphy triumphant, he slouches off muttering, "Didn't get my weight through." At such times it is important to remember the **Inviolate Law of Good Manners**: *it is forbidden to laugh at a golfer, no matter how grotesque his performance.*

Let us now follow the fortunes of four specific heroes—Stephen, Hugh, Doc and Leo. Three of them have been fiddling about, going through the usual preliminary rituals, but one of their members is missing.

"Where the hell is Leo," said Hugh, craning his neck toward the parking lot. "Has anyone seen him come in?"

"No," said Doc. "I don't know why he can't be on time once in a while."

"He lingers over-long in uxorious dalliance," said Stephen.

"Whatever that is, it doesn't do his game any good," said Hugh.

"Nothing will do his game any good."

"He'll come steaming up at the last minute in a sweaty swither, full of absurd excuses. He always does," said Doc.

"We're almost up," said Stephen. "Better toss for partners. Two close balls are together. Odd man with Leo."

"That'll make two of a kind on one team," said Hugh.

Stephen tossed three balls in the air. "Those two are partners," he said. "The Titleist is with Leo. That's you, Hugh."

"Oh, goody," said Hugh.

The Starter on the P.A. system announced: "Next on the tee will be Mr. Dedalus, Mr. Boylan, Dr. Lynch and Mr. Bloom. They will be followed by Mr. Tantalus, Mr. Sisyphus, Mr. Pandora and Mr. Hope."

"Hey, that's us," said Hugh. "We can't wait for Leo or we'll lose our place. He can catch up to us on the second, or wherever. I'll play with Harvey as a partner 'til he does. I'll be better off with Harvey than with Leo anyhow, despite his twenty-six strokes. Doc, you're up first.''

Doc shot a respectable 150 yards down the middle of the fairway; Stephen went a few yards past him; Hugh got a boomer of 225 yards. As the three of them were leaving the tee, a commotion along the path heralded the arrival of Leo. He came rushing along, dragging his clubs behind him, to the good-natured comments of the waiting golfers. "Speed it up, Leo, you just made it. Get going boy.''

Leo hurried up to Stephen. "The car wouldn't start and the traffic was unbelievable,'' he panted. "And—''

"We've hit,'' said Stephen. "You're up. Get going.''

"Okay,'' said Leo. He opened his ball pouch and a dozen balls fell out. He selected one and hurried out onto the tee.

(Oh why did I have to be late again everything happens to me tee up the ball not too high or excessive loft practice swing stiff as a board oh my head scalp too tight for the bone jiggle jiggle loosen up straight left arm what the hell has Molly got a bean up her ass about now I wasn't all that drunk just a few but oh my head slow back swing shift weight it's that red wine my guts are on fire ineluctable I never learn oh god let me get off this first tee after that I don't care all those eyes jiggle jiggle ball teed too low that's better practice swing stiff stiff look down fairway line up feet sand trap left Scylla trees right Charybdis straight down the strait what the blazes she sees in that guy I'll never know red wine oh what a bellyache change the grip right hand over that's better jiggle jiggle practice swing right elbow flew keep it in just let me get off this tee too close to ball heel it shuffle feet what's with Molly anyhow not ready to hit go anywhere except into those trees red wine never again left foot back bend knees keep head down no slice please no slice just let me get off this tee did last week jiggle jiggle bend knees red wine not too much got to hit it can't wait all those eyes got to hit it Molly you're a bitch WHACK there by god I hit it go straight no no it's starting to slice not those trees again hit something stay out of there it's deep in wouldn't you know it everything happens to me MULLIGAN!)

The overbearing malignity of Murphy on a golf course has led to the adoption of a compensatory rule carrying the name of another great Irishman, Mulligan. A Mulligan, for the uninitiated, is a dispensation to replay a bad shot without penalty. It is generally agreed by duffers that Mulligan has done more for golf than Vardon ever did. No one knows who Mulligan is or was, but generations of golfers have had reason to bless his name. In general, Mulligans are allowed only on the first tee (if allowed at all), with the idea in mind that a golfer's whole day should not be ruined by a disastrous start. This is not invariable—I had a golfer once tell me proudly that he had shot a ninety-six, but adding, "Not counting three Mulligans of course!" This seems a bit much and rather over-doing a good thing.

Mulligans are only awarded with the approval of opponents. If a golfer doesn't request a Mulligan, his opponents may say, "Better take a Mulligan," with specious sympathy and snide condescension. If a golfer accepts a Mulligan, either requested or offered, he has humbled himself before his enemies and will live under their largesse for the rest of the day. Another approach is for opponents to agree to a Mulligan but reserve that they have a "Mulligan-in-hand," to be used at their discretion later. They hope, of course that they won't need it and will be able to retain their moral superiority. This arrangement has something of the effect of a "gotcha"— the reserved right to goose a guy with a putter during his back-swing at an unspecified time. This is not generally approved.

For some reason, golfers seem to think that they need to holler "Mulligan" promptly. I've even known one golfer who shouted "Mulligan" during his back-swing, thereby assuring that he needed it.

The **Mulligan Tenet**: *a Mulligan is demeaning, unsportsmanlike and illegal, but you'll take it.*

A Mulligan can be a mixed blessing because of the **First Law of Bad Shots**: *one bad shot tends to generate another bad shot.* If the Mulligan shot is as bad as the first one, a golfer can't have another try—after all, he can't stand on the first tee and keep shooting until he gets a good one—he might be there all day.

Leo fell afoul of the First Law of Bad Shots and fired his second ball even deeper into the trees. He mumbled, "We'll find the first one," and trudged off to a day of terrible travail and serious suffering. This is fun?

OOO

The Fairway

OOO

Let us follow our four heroes as they leave the first tee and proceed on their odyssey during which they will demonstrate other laws of mischance. This record of laws will be cumulative in that some rules noted first in one situation may have application in others. For example, many of the laws of the first tee are pertinent to fairway play and vice versa. Leo has already demonstrated the **First Law of the Perversity of Inanimate Things**: *when addressing the ball, if you say or think "don't hit it over there," that's exactly where the ball will go.*

Hugh, who is a powerful big fellow, promptly demonstrated with his second shot, the **First Law of Long Hitters**: *if you hit a ball far enough it's sure to reach trouble.* Big men get their jollies from knocking the ball a country mile and to hell with accuracy.

"Hitting the ball smack on the screws is the second greatest joy in the world," said Hugh.

"You should know," said Doc. "You're a devotee of both."

"It doesn't work for me," said Stephen. "The **Rule of Negative Returns** states: *the harder the swing, the shorter the shot.*"

"I know," said Leo.

"I'd better hit a provisional," said Hugh.

A provisional ball is different from a Mulligan—for one thing, it's legitimate. If the player finds the first ball, he plays it; if he does not, then he plays the provisional ball with a penalty. If the provisional ball follows the first ball into the trees, as is common, then the player has the advantage of looking for two balls. A little vagueness about the make and number of the balls being played provides a further advantage. The **Law of Provisional Balls**: *an opponent looking for a first ball and a provisional ball in the same area always finds the first ball.*

On the second hole, Doc gave a demonstration of the **Law of the Unworkable Hypothesis**: *if your drive is short, you must hit the second shot twice as hard to make up the distance, your third shot must be hit three times as hard, and so on.* This sequence is self-defeating and complementary to the Rule of Negative Returns.

On the third hole Leo got a good drive down the

middle of the fairway. When he reached the ball it was sitting in a deep divot hole.

"Are we playing WFR?" asked Leo.

"Winter rules in July?" said Doc.

"How come," complained Leo, "that when I'm faced with five thousand square yards of smooth grass, my ball finds the only deep divot hole?"

"You have no problem," said Doc. "You have the great good fortune of being short-sighted. I have observed that you therefore find it necessary to pick up your ball to identify it. The fact that the ball seldom gets returned to its original position is, I am sure, accidental. We shall all turn our backs while you identify your ball."

"Golf builds character," said Stephen. "It trains you to meet the vicissitudes of life by teaching you how to cheat—and to live with it."

"Golf suborns," said Doc.

"I don't cheat," said Leo.

"All golfers cheat," said Hugh.

"Honesty is the last resort of the emotionally insecure," said Stephen.

By the time our friends had reached the fourth hole they became aware of the **First Law of Slow Play**: *the foursome ahead will be slow players, the foursome behind will be fast.* Slow play, by others, is the bane of all golfers. "By others" is the key phrase here. No golfer believes that he himself is slow. I've never talked to a golfer yet who didn't claim that he played very quickly and could complete a round in two-and-a-half

hours if there were nobody ahead of him. But he will have a diatribe ready about the moribund play of others—even the members of his own foursome.

Slow play has a deleterious effect on performance. When you have been forced to wait interminably for those ahead to get out of range, you can be sure you will get a flub, despite (or because of) the opportunity to take innumerable practice swings. The **Second Law of Slow Play**: *the longer you have to wait to take a shot, the worse it will be.* A bad shot exacerbates the exasperation with the slow play, which screws things up even worse, which...but need we go on? Golfers have been known to froth at the mouth when held up unduly on a round, which has a disastrous effect on performance, as evidenced by the **Frothing Law**: *hitting a ball while frothing at the mouth is not conducive to a good shot.*

When our group arrived on the fifth tee, the foursome ahead had hit their drives 160 yards down the fairway and were waiting patiently to take their second shots to the green 275 yards away, on which some golfers were still visible.

"What the hell are they waiting for?" said Stephen. "Old Garfinkle couldn't reach the green from there with a cannon."

"We would have to get behind the Geritol set of four past-presidents," said Doc. "Someone should put Tabasco on their jockstraps."

"Past-presidents figure they own the course and stickhandle down the fairway like the Bryn Mawr grass hockey team. Ordinary rules don't apply to them," said Stephen.

"One thing for sure," said Hugh, "they won't be discussing women."

"If Garfinkle was wearing a codpiece, he should put it on his head," said Doc.

"Garfinkle beat Doc once in a tournament and he's never forgiven him," said Stephen.

"If he had pruritus ani he'd be itchy all over," said Doc.

During the round to that point, our friends had, perforce, held up the foursome behind them on every hole. These worthies had resorted to the standard manifestations of impatience: standing with arms akimbo, glaring down the fairway, irritable practice swings, sitting on the wheels of their carts, and finally, lying sleeping on the grass. Broad hints, you might say.

At the first opportunity, when the two rear foursomes impinged, Hugh said, "Those donkeys ahead are holding up the whole course."

"Yeah," said Tantalus. "Somebody is."

On the average, four people can play down a five-hundred-yard fairway faster than four people can hole-out once they reach the green. Therefore, delays are more apparent when waiting for putters on the green. Other players are always interminable in their putting; your group is fast. Ask any golfer. Impatience can overcome judgement.

On the seventh hole, our friends had taken their drives and were gazing down the fairway at the distant green where the past-presidents were wandering about in a relaxed fashion.

"What the blazes are they doing?" said Stephen. "Holding a convention?"

"They must be playing for a dollar a stroke," said Hugh.

"Not old Garfinkle," said Doc. "He's as tight as a bull's arse in fly time."

It was Leo's turn to hit. While he waited he took six practice swings; he walked around in circles; he took six more practice swings; he stared at the figures on the green.

"Without being derogatory," said Doc finally, "I think you can hit, Leo."

"I guess so," said Leo. He took three more practice swings then swung easily at the ball. The ball took off like a rocket. The four of them stood in open-mouthed amazement as the ball flew in a beautiful arc straight for the pin. It landed at the front of the green, skittered forward to run between Mr. Garfinkle's feet as he was making his putt. That worthy stabbed his putt ten feet past the hole, then whirled to stare down the fairway in utter disbelief.

"Fore," shouted Leo. Then, with great presence of mind he pointed at Doc.

"You bastard," said Doc. "I'll give you a prostatic massage with a five iron."

"It was your fault," said Leo. "You told me to shoot."

"I didn't expect a bloody miracle!" roared Doc.

"You picked a great group to shoot into," said Hugh. "Four past-presidents, all infamous for their irascible tempers. Too bad, Leo, we'll miss you around here."

"I understand there's a share available at Broadbend," said Stephen. "Better grab it, Leo."

"You can be sure the Rules Committee will hear about this solecism," said Doc. "And that Committee is in the hip pocket of the past-presidents—all the better for ass-kissing purposes. And don't try to point the finger at me again, either."

"Well, they've been holding us up all day," said Leo. "Maybe I'll beat them to the gun by sending in a complaint to the Rules Committee about their slow play."

"**McManus Maxim**: never stand behind a coughing cow in weed time," said Doc.

On the next hole, *mirabile dictu,* the unthinkable happened—the past-presidents invited our friends to play through.

"What are they up to," murmured Hugh. "They haven't allowed anyone to play through them in twenty years."

"Maybe they want to have a shot at Leo," said Stephen.

"No, they just want to identify him for lynching purposes," said Doc.

Leo's profuse and obsequious apologies to the past-presidents about shooting into them were received with frigid politeness.

Our heroes took their shots, as invited, and ran

head-on into the **First Law of Playing Through**: *when playing through another foursome, the possibility of getting a good shot is negligible.* Stephen hooked into a bunker, Leo sliced into the trees, Doc sculled his shot about twenty yards, and Hugh dug a divot as big as a tam-o'-shanter.

"You don't mind if we carry on," said Mr. Garfinkle.

"Please do," said Doc.

The past-presidents smiled sweetly and continued on their way.

Thus our friends blew their opportunity to get back to the bar an hour earlier.

"Infukinevitable," said Hugh.

OOO

The Rough

OOO

Golf clubs expend a great deal of effort and money grooming the fairways, which is wasted on duffers because they spend most of their time elsewhere. The elsewhere is called the rough—and frequently more descriptive things. The rough looks very pretty, from outside, with all its trees, bushes, flowers, and charming greenery. But from inside, your perspective changes and it becomes an ugly, perverse monstrosity. The **First Rough Rule** reads: *the rough is a good place not to be.* **Corollary 1**: *the harder you try to stay out of the rough, the more it doesn't work.*

The way to keep out of the rough is to shoot straight down the middle of the fairway. This is impossible or fairways would only need to be ten feet wide. The width of the fairway is therefore designed to allow some latitude in straying—but it is never wide enough. Sooner or later you're going to end up in the rough, so you might as well be reconciled to it and plan accordingly.

The malevolence of Murphy is particularly manifest in the rough because the possibility of things going awry therein goes up enormously. Murphy loves the rough.

The laws of mischance relative to the rough can be broken down into two categories: (i) getting in, and (ii) getting out.

Getting In. There's no trick to getting into the rough—it's the getting out that poses problems. Various manifestations of Murphy will send the ball heading for the bush: slicing, hooking, duck-hooking, grunching, toeing, heeling, and so forth. A player will find other explanations such as a "bad bounce," although how a ball can be deflected by a blade of grass is not quite clear.

The **Second Rough Rule** is: *your ball will always slice, except when the trees are on the left, at which time it will hook (or vice versa).* **Corollary 1**: *if you allow for your usual slice (or hook), you won't get it.*

There are a number of laws which take into account the discriminative manifestations of the Murphy syndrome. One such example which relates to the rough is the **First Law of Selective Perversity**: *your ball when shot into the trees will inevitably find a place behind a large tree or* *where you can't get a swing at it; your opponent's ball when shot into the trees, will bounce back onto the fairway, or at the very least, will land in an open, playable lie.*

When your ball has ended up in the trees, the first thing you have to do is to find the goddamned thing. This exercise is a midway step between "getting in" and "getting out." There are a number of laws apropos to this frustrating experience. The **First Law of Ball Finding**: *never look for a ball where you hope it will be; it won't be there.* You might as well accept the fact that it will be in the worst possible situation.

Your so-called friends will eventually come to help you look for your ball, after ignoring you for as long as possible. There are a number of rules governing their behaviour. The **Second Law of Ball Finding**: *your friends will get tired of looking for your ball before you do.* **Corollary 1**: *your opponent, looking for his ball, will keep up the search indefinitely.* The official rules have a regulation about the length of time that can be spent looking for a ball, but your opponent never remembers it when looking for his ball. He recalls it clearly when looking for yours.

There are certain games people play in ball-finding. As a demonstration, let us look in on a search for Leo's ball in the woods.

"Here's a ball," said Hugh. "It's a Titleist 4. Is that yours, Leo?" You will notice that Hugh has identified the ball, which gives Leo a chance to claim it. Hugh is Leo's partner and has a vested interest in helping Leo find his ball—or at least, a ball, any ball. "It's in the middle of a bush," added Hugh, helpfully. Leo immediately disclaimed ownership.

Ordinarily, when you find a ball which might be your opponent's, you ask him what he is playing rather than saying what you have found. This implies, ever so faintly, that you don't trust him. Also, it commits him to a particular ball. Doc, however, came up with a trap-play variation.

"Here's a ball," said Doc. "It's a Hogan 3. Is that yours, Leo?"

Leo isn't playing a Hogan 3, but in the interests of, ahem, saving time, he is prepared to accept this as his ball.

"Yes," said Leo.

After a short pause, Doc spoke again. "Oh, sorry, it's a ProStaff 3."

A ProStaff 3 is what Leo was playing. In Doc's terminology, this puts Leo on the horns of an enema. If he doesn't claim the ball, he will be penalized two strokes; if he does, after saying he was playing a Hogan 3, he is highly suspect. He made up his mind with lightning rapidity.

"Yes, I was playing a ProStaff 3," said Leo. "I changed my ball on the last tee. I forgot."

"Make up your mind, Leo," said Doc, kicking Leo's ball behind a tree.

When Leo came forward, Doc pointed out the ball to him. Leo looked sadly at the tree.

"Isn't that a planted tree?" asked Leo.

"No," said Doc. "The **Rule on Planted Trees** states: *if a tree is over a hundred feet high, and/or has a diameter of over a foot, it isn't a planted tree.* That tree has been there since the Pleistocene era. And don't pee on the ball and claim casual water, either."

When they had holed out, Leo said, "I don't know if I had a six or a seven."

"You had a nine," said Doc. "With a bit of charity thrown in."

On the next hole, retribution—Doc's ball was in the trees. After a lengthy period of searching, Doc said sadly, "You fellows go ahead. I'll look a bit longer and if I don't find it I'll pick up." He doesn't really mean it and hopes they will insist on continuing the search. His friends take off immediately. However, they haven't gone twenty-five yards when Doc calls out, "Here it is." And a ball comes flying out from the depths of the woods.

The deep woods lends itself well to chicanery. The **Law of Seduction** states: *a bad lie tends to corrupt; an absolutely terrible lie corrupts absolutely.* In the trees, shots with intent are indistinguishable from practice swings; a missed shot can masquerade as an effort to clear away grass or bushes; a fast bit of footwork does wonders for a bad lie; a gentle poke with the clubhead can improve the situation enormously; hand-mashies are not unknown. It is considered unethical to toss out a new ball surreptitiously—the hole in the pocket is

passé—but a found ball is open season. Maybe you did forget what you were playing. Maybe it was a Lynx 7 and not a Tourney 2. After all, you deserve the benefit of the doubt, don't you? Of course you do.

Getting Out. We have considered certain aspects of getting out of the rough, but let us go into the matter in more depth. The deep rough is called "Tiger Country" or being "Up to Your Ass in Alligators." Conflicting terms, perhaps, but both apt. In Tiger Country, the Laws of the Jungle prevail.

If you think, wherever you are, that the situation couldn't get worse, you are wrong. The **First Law of the Jungle** (also known as the **Domino Theory of Escalating Disasters**) states: *no matter how bad the situation is, it will get worse; this is progressive to the nth power.* (Pick-up time. Score x.)

It is difficult for a golfer to accept the **Second Law of the Jungle**: *one bad shot is going to cost you a minimum of three.* One into the jungle, one to get out, and one to recover. That's a bare-boned minimum and assumes that Murphy will turn his back—which is very unlikely. A golfer will try to circumvent this inexorable penalty by a long, brilliant recovery shot. Your opponent may carry it off, but you won't. No way. The jungle will have its due. Inexorable.

The official rules, with great good sense, accept

the fact that a ball may end up in an impossible situation. They offer the dispensation of moving the ball two club-lengths, not nearer the hole, for a one-stroke penalty. Cut your losses, say the rules. Few golfers have the good sense to use the dispensation; they get greedy and try for a little extra distance. They figure that with a little bit of luck they can certainly do better than the two club-lengths and maybe a great deal better. Forlorn.

A case has been made for shooting through trees on the basis that a tree has more air spaces than solid material and therefore you have a good chance of being successful. This theory seems to be valid for your opponents, whose shots can consistently thread through a maze of trees without hazard. But for you, the **Third Law of the Jungle** applies: *in a shot through the trees, your ball will clear everything, except the last branch.* One factor to be kept in mind relative to the air-hole theory is that trees on golf courses have prehensile branches which can reach out, grab a ball and fling it back into the rough. I've seen it happen many a time.

Another example of the sneaky participation of tree branches in golf shots is to be found when the tree is behind you. A practice swing will disclose that your back-swing will clear the tree easily. But when you take your shot, the branch will reach out and deflect your club. It's the only possible explanation.

On the twelfth hole Hugh was in the trees. Hugh

was a strong hitter and something of a gambler. He looked sourly at the ball.

(There you are you misbegotten spheroid wouldn't you know it a half inch to the left and off the tree onto fairway but not me a foot shorter and a clear shot good game ruined maybe not Doc watching me can't move it chip back to fairway blow score two club lengths not good enough let me see green through there could reach 175 yards easy between those two trees hook over those evergreens back in the game ball sitting up lousy back swing shorten up club punch it four wood no four iron loft hit hard to clear take a ride sweetheart powder it here goes WHACK got it BONK BONK THUNK.)

"Where did it go?" shouted Hugh.

"It hit a tree and bounced over your head into the woods behind you," said Doc. "Tough luck."

"Wouldn't you know it," said Hugh. "Some days you can't pee a drop."

○○○
Sand Traps
& Water Hazards
○○○

Sand traps and water hazards are regrettable vestiges left over from the early days of golf. The first golf courses were links on the seashores of Scotland where sand and water abounded. When golf became respectable and moved inland, the absurd tradition of sand and water came along with it. Duffers have had ample reason to curse golf's genesis.

Sand Traps. We shall discuss the dilemma occasioned by sand traps from two aspects, as we did when considering the rough, *i.e.*, (i) getting in, and (ii) getting out.

As with the rough, there is no difficulty about getting in—in fact it is practically impossible not to do so if there is a trap anywhere in your vicinity.

Balls have a remarkable affinity for sand traps; or, putting it another way, sand has an extraordinary attraction for balls. This attraction has something to do with a little understood natural physical phenomenon involving variable gravity and/or fluctuating magnetism. A ball will be sailing along, avoiding the trap nicely, when it will suddenly veer off sharply in the direction of the trap. Sand, obviously, has a mega-magnetic pull on rubber spheroids. Sand is only exceeded in this respect by water.

The scientific explanation for this phenomenon is dependent upon the well-known attraction between particles. Sand comprises an infinite number of tiny constituents, each one sending out currents of attraction. Although the force exerted by any one element is minute, when it is multiplied by the astronomical number of particles, the product is formidable. If the sand were combined into one rock, you would have no trouble avoiding it, but with sand traps it's a different kettle of fish. Therefore, around traps, the usual forces of gravity and magnetism are sharply intensified.

Preliminary work in our laboratory has developed the following formula in an effort to quantify the phenomenon:

$$A = \frac{n^2 \times b \times M \times ff}{-sk}$$

A = attraction between ball and trap, expressed in Murphs

n = number of particles of sand, which is infinite (n^2 is even bigger)

b = ball weight in milligrams

M = Murphy force (a substantial component in this situation)

ff = fudge factor (used in some form or other in all scientific formulae)

sk = skill of golfer (a negative figure).

A simple formula, but it sure explains a lot.

Observe now the formula in operation. I have already described the tangential swerve induced by a trap when a ball is flying near it. The force is so strong that the ball will turn almost at right angles to get into the trap. You will hit the ball with more than enough force to carry the trap. But the ball at its apogee over the trap will begin to hover and then plunge right down into the sand. The synergistic contribution of the M force is epitomized in the **First Law of Sand Traps**: *when shooting over a sand trap, the ball will clear the trap, except the last two inches.*

You often find that greens are set up with sand traps on two sides, across from one another. This arrangement frequently results in a ping pong effect, back and forth from one to the other and back again. From this series of events we derive the **Second Law of Sand Traps**: *a sand trap across the green from the one you are in increases the probability of sculling your shot.* **Corollary 1**: *on any return shot, the probability of sculling*

once again goes up exponentially. If, by some miracle, your ball lands on the green, the powerful attractive force of the trap on the other side will suck the ball across the green into its gritty embrace.

When a ball lands in a trap from a considerable height it tends to bury itself in the sand. The declivity so formed is called a "fried egg." Shooting out of a fried egg makes an impossible shot even more so. If there is a foot mark anywhere in the trap then the **Third Law of Sand Traps** comes into play: *your ball will land in a foot mark, if one is available.* This fate is manifestly unjust because of the **First Law of Unfairness**: *you always rake sand traps; other people don't.* Piteous bleats to your associates for relief from this victimization are treated with the disdain they deserve. You have to play her where she lies—if anyone is watching.

Once you've arrived in a sand trap the objective from then on is to get out—somehow, somewhere, anywhere, but preferably on the green. Good golfers will tell you that getting out of a sand trap is the easiest shot in golf. That's balderdash—it's the hardest. The average golfer enters a sand trap with a feeling of horror; he's convinced he won't get out with one shot. The influence of mind over matter is a strong factor in this situation, as evidenced by the **First Law of Positive Negative Thinking**: *if a golfer is positive he won't get out of a sand trap, he won't.* The **Second Law of Positive**

Negative Thinking reads: *if he is positive he will get out, he won't anyhow.*

Leo was in a trap at the side of the green on the eleventh.

(Wouldn't you know it no reason to be in here shot for the other side no way I can get out maybe maybe not a big swing ball just sitting there in the open no problem just plop it up onto the green only a few feet just a little tap pick it off gently why didn't it stay on the grass trickled in one foot did it my kind of luck subtle chip don't need much of a swing just a little tap and up she goes there swing tap oh hell six inches.)

"You've got to blast it, Leo," said Hugh.

The problem with a blast shot is judging the amount of sand to take. Leo ground his feet into the sand up to his ankles, wiggled and waggled, closed his eyes and took a wild swipe at the ball. He showered the surrounding area and his face with a cloud of sand. The ball hopped another six inches.

"Too much sand," said Hugh. "Just two inches behind the ball."

"Okay," said Leo.

He repeated the performance, taking a full, hard swing. This time he got no sand at all. The ball flew across the green into the trees a hundred yards beyond.

"Your best drive of the day," said Doc. "We'll see you on the next tee, Leo."

"The bottom just fell out of your garbage bag, Leo," said Stephen.

A special sort of club has been designed for sand trap shots, which is called appropriately a "sand wedge." The sand wedge is a heavy club which could be used to split a curling rock but seldom has enough power to move a 1.6 ounce ball six feet. The club has enough loft to cause the ball to fly up and hit you in the crotch if you're not careful. However, duffers subscribe consistently and persistently to the **First Scooping Law**: *never trust the loft of a club to do the job; always help it by scooping.* This law is in direct conflict with the **Second Scooping Law**: *scooping a shot doesn't help.* Once again we see a law of practice (intrinsic) in conflict with a law of analysis (extrinsic). Duffers will continue to follow the First Scooping Law because the motivation is obsessive, despite the overwhelming evidence in support of the Second Scooping Law. Therefore, scooping is here to stay.

Pros recommend that golfers spend a lot of time in the practice sand traps. The thing to do is to throw a hundred balls into one of these sand pits and whang away at them. If you get one onto the green, quit—the problem is solved.

If you continue to have difficulty mastering the sand wedge then an option open to you, when the lip is less than six inches, is to use a putter. When employed in this way, a putter is called a Texas Wedge, a Mayfair Wedge, or sometimes a Chicken Sand Wedge.

In the meantime, until the official rules take the sensible step of approving a set of long tongs for getting out of sand traps, the thing to do when you get into one of these obscene bunkers is to declare the ball unplayable, throw it out on the grass and accept a one-stroke penalty. You'll be money ahead in the long run.

Water Holes. The principal role of water holes is to take balls out of circulation so the pro can sell more golf balls. An additional advantage to the pro is that when the water is drained, he gets hundreds of balls for the practice fairway, and a few to sell as "seconds."

Water holes are an all-or-nothing proposition— your ball is either in the water or it isn't. The usual factors producing entry are applicable, but the problem of getting out doesn't arise. There used to be a ball called a "floater" but the idea seems to have sunk. I never could figure out how you would hit a floating ball anyhow—unless you were a senior prelate or a politician.

I have made reference to the strong attractive power which water exerts on a golf ball when we were discussing sand traps. Water power is even more puissant than that of sand because of the supra-infinite number of molecules in water, each exerting an attractive force.

The penalty for going into the water differs depending on whether your ball went in directly, hit something on the other side and fell back, or entered laterally. Interpretation of these regulations has started more arguments than any other golfing topic, with the possible exception of the question as to whether blondes are sexier than brunettes. I have no advice to offer on either subject.

If your ball does go into the water, you then discover the **Not Quite Rule**: *a ball in the water is just beyond the reach of your ball retriever.* Relying on your friend to hold your hand so you can stretch that extra eighteen inches is not without hazard if he has a sense of humour. Brave, or parsimonious, golfers will sometimes take off their shoes and socks and wade in, but don't do it if someone in the foursome has a camera—your picture will end up on the notice board.

"What should I use?" asked Leo, looking out over the pond on the fifteenth.

"An old ball," said Doc, "to quote the classical reply."

"Why are you getting out your ball retriever, Leo?" asked Hugh. "You haven't shot yet."

"He's been here before," said Stephen.

"Another example of the power of positive thinking," said Doc.

Leo teed up his ball, averted his eyes from the water and swung. The ball skipped six times on the water, rolled up the bank and came to rest a foot from the hole.

"Nice shot," said Doc. "You'll have to show me how to do it some day, Leo."

"Put on lots of over-spin," said Leo.

◯◯◯

Putting

◯◯◯

Once you reach the green you are involved in the ignoble art of putting. It is a travesty of human endeavour to see a two-hundred-pound athlete crouched like a defecating spaniel, sweat dripping off his nose, muscles in rigor, nerves twitching, teeth clenched, endeavouring to move a tiny ball ten feet. He is closely observed in his absurd travail by three other stalwarts standing as still as cigar store Indians. No one moves a muscle, no one takes a breath, until the act is consummated. Then another competitor repeats the performance.

Murphy plays a big role in putting—balls rim the cup, go in and then jump out, go straight for the hole and then veer off, sit on the edge held up by one blade of grass, or go right over the hole, defying the laws of gravity. It's unbelievable what Murphy can do to a putt until you've witnessed it. The selective enmity of Murphy is particularly manifest in putts—your ball will stay out, your opponent's will flub in. His ball will spin around the hole and come in the back door, at which point he will invariably say, ''Never in doubt.''

The principal problem in putting is that there is no attraction between the ball and the hole. A hole is by definition empty, so there are no particles therein to suck the ball into the hole. Indeed, there appears to be a negative effect which has never been seriously investigated, although frequently commented on—loudly and profanely.

Each golfer has his own unique style of putting—weight on left or right foot or equally distributed; low crouch or upright stance; grip over or under; index finger along the shaft or wrapped around; elbows in or out; and so forth. Also, the preliminary manoeuvres to determine distance and side roll are very personal exercises which cannot be hurried. When you consider that this charade is perpetrated in a foursome on an average of at least eight times on every hole, you can understand why a convention appears to be in progress on the green. The futility of all this nonsense is summarized in the **First Law of Putting**: *the longer the fidget, the less chance there is of sinking the putt.*

Leo was preparing to putt on the undulating twelfth green.

''We shall now witness the mating dance of the concupiscent flamingo,'' murmured Doc.

Leo circled the hole, examining the situation from the four points of the compass, squatting and squinting and holding up his club as a plumb-bob.

"Who's your choreographer, Leo?" asked Doc.

"The mind is a computer," said Leo, "accepting data relative to distance, direction, up or down hill and side roll and then programming the muscles to perform appropriately."

"A classic case of garbage in, garbage out," said Stephen.

Leo returned to his ball, took three practice swings and then paused. "There's a lady-bug on my ball," he complained.

"She's probably gone to sleep," said Doc.

"Tell her to fly away home, her house is on fire and her children will burn," said Stephen.

Leo marked his ball, picked it up and blew at the lady-bug, saying, "Shoo, shoo." The bug thereupon flew up his nose. Leo went stomping around the green in a paroxysm of sneezing and snorting, to the delight of his friends. Who says Murphy doesn't have a sense of humour?

"I always suspected that chivalry was wasted on lady-bugs," said Stephen.

Leo replaced his ball, took three practice swings and then knocked the ball six feet beyond the cup.

"Pshaw," said Leo.

"Watch your language," said Stephen.

"I haven't heard anybody say 'pshaw' in twenty years," said Doc.

"It's better than pshit," said Hugh.

Leo was short on the return putt, thereby completing a demonstration of two basic laws of putting. Some idiot, years ago, promulgated a truism in the **Apodictic Law of Putting**: *never up, never in*. As a result of this law, duffers tend to hit the ball well beyond the hole. Leo also fell afoul of the **Law of Over-Compensation**: *if you are long on your first putt, you will be short on the next one; and vice versa.*

In an effort to reduce the delay caused by putting, the practice of conceding short putts has been adopted in informal play. These are called "gimmes". This custom opens up new parameters of mischief. The **First Law of Gimmes** states: *a golfer is keener to save time by conceding his own putts than those of his opponents.* An **Extension** of this law reads: *a partner is more generous at conceding putts than an opponent.*

There is considerable variation in the distance at which gimmes are awarded, depending on a number of factors. For example, if it is a fourth putt, the distance tolerated would probably be greater than that on an earlier one. However, under such a circumstance, the conceder will ostentatiously knock the ball away and say, "You've suffered enough." The length of putt conceded tends to increase as a game goes on. This generosity may come to an abrupt halt. After conceding several fairly long putts, an opponent may all of a sudden be found gazing off into the distance when his colleague is facing a short putt of importance. The putter will fuss around waiting for his friend to notice, but he will be ignored. Finally in annoyance, the putter will stomp up to the putt—and miss it. This was planned all along. The **Rule of Complaint** says: *you have no complaint to your opponent if you miss a short putt* (he was right in requiring you to putt); *but you can pretend to a complaint of you make it.* Golfers invariably reverse this protocol.

Putts are sometimes conceded for unstated future considerations. This ploy usually involves conceding putts which mean nothing at a considerable distance. For example, a putt for an eight may be given fairly generously by an opponent who has already holed-out in five. The anticipation is that a similar distance will be approved in the future when the conceder is putting for a par. This seldom works despite broad hints such as, "I've got my hearing aid turned up but I don't hear anything."

In an effort to standardize the length of gimmes, the concept of conceding "within the leather" has been introduced. However, this procedure promptly resulted in the appearance of putters as long as drivers, with two inches of leather for a grip. A foursome, to circumvent this chicanery, will usually designate one club in the group to serve as the measuring device. If the "within the leather" rule is adhered to, you run into the **Second Law of Gimmes**: *your ball will be just beyond the leather; your opponent's ball will be just within.*

One thing to watch for, if your opponent is doing

the measuring, is to make sure the club head is at the front of the hole. If he pushes it to the back of the cup, then you have lost four-and-a-half inches, which may make the difference between a gimme and a knee-knocker.

There are ways your opponent will use to circumvent the "within the leather" criterion. The most common procedure is for him to rely on his kindly, generous eye. He will state, "That's obviously within the leather" and knock the ball away. No challenge is then possible. Another device I have seen used, when a ball has been hit overly hard, is to reach across the hole and stop the ball, even if, or particularly if, it is scooting along like a scared rabbit. The implication is that it was going to stop within the leather; if that were indeed true, there would have been no necessity to stop it. There is no defence against this sort of thing beyond invoking the two-stroke penalty for hitting a moving ball, which might get you a split lip. The only thing to do in dealing with gimme manoeuvring is to follow the **Lex Romano**: *when in Rome, eat spaghetti.*

Another bit of chicanery to be alert to has to do with ball markers. If your opponent puts the marker in front of the ball and then replaces the ball ahead of the marker, he has picked up about two inches. If his ball is very dirty and has to be cleaned three times then he can move forward six inches. This hinching may be accidental, but I've never seen a ball placed farther from the hole than it was to start with, which raises a faint suspicion.

Quite frequently a golfer who has missed a putt will bring the ball back and take a practice putt over again. The **Rule of Second Putts** states: *on a second try at a missed putt, when it doesn't count, the ball will always go in the hole.*

So great is the strain of putting on the nervous system that some golfers develop what is know as the "yips"—a convulsive jump at the ball instead of a smooth stroke. The yips are a very real thing and a horror to behold. While in the toils of the yips, a player may miss the ball completely, stub it an inch, or wallop it right off the green. I've even seen a yipper hit the ball three times in one shot with a series of spasmodic jerks. Even if a yipper does't yip a particular shot he will be so afraid of doing so that his putting will go all to hell. The yips are no respecters of persons and may afflict good players as well as duffers. It is obvious that the yips are a favourite tool of Murphy if the rest of your game is going well. The **First Law of Yips**: *the yips come from we know not where and descend with equal virulence upon the just (yourself) and the unjust (your opponent).* However, a certain degree of preconditioning is not infrequently a factor in the yips. The **Second Law of the Yips**: *the incidence of the yips is directly proportional to the amount of booze consumed the night before.*

To deal with the yips, or indeed with other situations where a golfer's putting has gone really sour, he may resort to a variety of extreme mea-

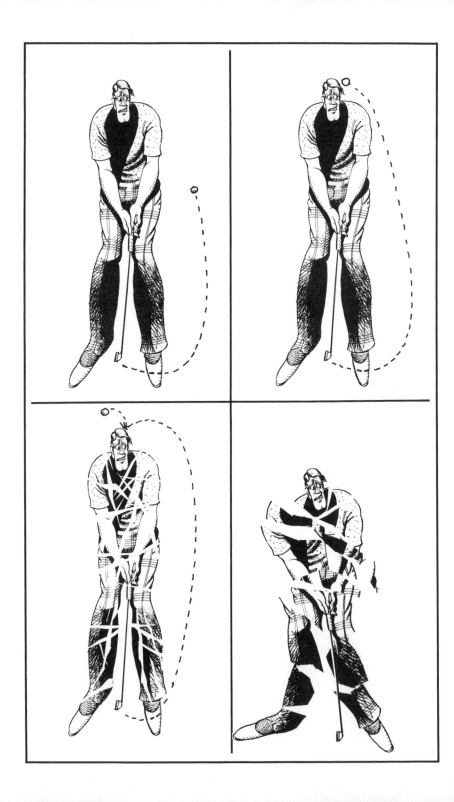

sures, such as: putting with one hand, or left-handed, or cross-handed; or between the legs (illegal); or from directly behind the ball; or yoga. None of these accomplish much except to amuse your friends. The yips may depart as suddenly as they came, but until they do, life is hell.

Putting is very important—you can't score if you don't putt well. There's a good deal of truth in the old adage that you "drive for show and you putt for dough." A two-inch putt costs the same as a 250-yard drive, which doesn't seem fair, but that's golf. The importance of a shot, particularly a putt, increases as the game progresses, until on the eighteenth the whole match and the financial stake related thereto often rides on a single putt. Your opponents will be very helpful in pointing this out to you in case you had overlooked it. The **Final Law of Putting**: *the difficulty of making a putt is directly proportional to the number of bets riding on it.*

Equipment

A golfer in the Pro Shop is like a kid in a candy factory. What an exciting display of the trappings and paraphernalia of golf! As far as price is concerned, avert the eyes. Since you're plunking out a big pile of moola to play golf anyhow, you owe it to yourself not to go chintzy on the back-up stuff. Splurge.

Let us consider first of all the matter of clothes. The **First Law of Golfing Haberdashery** states: *it is essential that you look like a golfer, whether or not you are one.* In your ordinary work-a-day world you may be limited by your vocation to a pin-stripe suit or overalls, which doesn't give you much room for artistic expression. But in choosing your golfing togs you can discard the cloak of the mundane and give free rein to your latent sense of flamboyant elegance. Throw off your inhibitions—let your imagination soar. Anything goes—reds, greens, purples, variegated—you name it, Gary Player notwithstanding. As a result, the first tee frequently rivals the Lido chorus line (excluding the upper part) in resplendent finery. Don't let your wife buy your golfing clothes. If you do, you will save a lot of money but you won't look like a golfer—you'll look like an accountant playing golf. It's a great pity that plus-fours are temporarily out of style, as they were the ultimate in sartorial elegance. Maybe you could lead the way in their return. Go ahead. I'll dare you.

Next, the head-gear. This can be nearly anything except a fedora or a coon-skin hat. The ''in thing'' these days is to wear a cap bearing the name of some famous exotic club, whether or not you have ever been there. You can get Elvin to bring one back for you. Such a cap gives you the panache of a well-travelled golfer. Some golfers who really have travelled extensively may indulge in reverse snobbery by wearing a cap emblazoned ODEON TRACTORS, but if you work for that firm don't wear it—unless you're playing with the boss. Reverse snobbery is only for those who have a snobbery to put in reverse.

If your shoes didn't cost at least a hundred and fifty dollars you are out of step with modern swank golfers. The way to draw attention to your splendid shoes is to complain bitterly to your colleagues about what they cost. However, this will elicit similar complaints from others, whose shoes invariably cost more than yours did.

Don't fuss unduly about your choice of a golf ball. Golf balls are round, dimpled and fickle—which may remind you of another species. You can ignore claims by manufacturers about long distance, wearing qualities, and accuracy. These matters are irrelevant. What you really need to do is to find a friendly ball—one which is not a mole for Murphy. Balls are sometimes on your side, unlike clubs which are consistently and perversely agin' you. If you do discover a friendly ball, cherish it. I've known golfers who have found a co-operative ball to play with it 'til the cover falls off. The first manufacturer who advertises "friendly balls" will make a mint. However, even a friendly ball is fickle and may turn against you at the most inauspicious moment. You just have to be tolerant. Golf is one of the few sports where you don't share a ball with someone else, as you do in baseball, polo, tennis, and marbles. It's yours and yours alone. If you do inadvertently share someone else's ball, it will cost you the hole.

Most golfers don't like to play with balls on which their names are imprinted. A golfer never buys them for himself but is frequently given a dozen by his wife for Father's Day or some other pagan celebration. She thinks it's a real swanky gimmick. The reluctance to use such balls arises from the fact that when you lose a ball, you do so some place where you would rather nobody knew you've been. You will probably get your ball back—a plus—but at some cost to your pride. The **Rule of Prodigal Balls** states: *your monogrammed ball will always be found by a loudmouth.* He will come over to you in the bar and say so everyone can hear, "Look what I found a hundred yards into the trees on the third. What the hell were you doing there?" Your reply that you were looking for mushrooms or picking blueberries is not persuasive. If you try to turn the tables on him by asking him what he himself was doing there, he will say he was looking for Ralph's ball (and, knowing Ralph, this is highly credible). But this excuse is not open to you because your name is on the ball. No. Let your balls be incognito.

Your bag, which must be as big as a steamer trunk, should be festooned with status symbols and fully stocked with golfing gear. The whole thing weighs about a hundred pounds. Let us examine Hugh Boylan's equipment as an example of an average golfer's bag. Dangling from the straps are plastic medallions from a considerable number of prestigious clubs, including the Pro-Am tournament at Moose Jaw, an airline tag reading Tokyo, and a rabbit's foot charm. Attached to the bag are an umbrella, a towel, a ball retriever, a shooting stick, and a sweater. The club covers look like bedroom slippers from a seraglio. A partial inventory of the pockets discloses: three new balls and eighty-five scruffies; a plethora of tees and ball markers; one good glove and seven that are stiff and dried out; five pencils; several old score cards; a rain suit; a sweater; a wind-breaker; one sock with a hole in it; a chocolate bar which has melted and phagocytosed several tees and ball markers; mosquito repellant; a box of aspirin; three Sheiks; a tube of pile ointment; a package of Tums; corn pads; an empty bottle of suntan lotion; band-aids; several silver coins; a set of keys that were misplaced a year ago; a tube of Nivea; a shoe-shine kit; and a mickey of scotch.

Hugh is obviously the complete golfer, ready for every eventuality.

The pro will be happy to set you up with all these accoutrements so that, when you take your place on the tee, observers will recognize that you are a golfer to be reckoned with—until you take your first shot.

The altruistic service which a pro provides in encouraging golfers to buy good and therefore expensive equipment invariably leads to complaints that he is more interested in money than in golf. What's wrong with that? Is a dentist in love with teeth? Are plumbers really all that fond of toilets? Does a stockbroker regard a bond as a work of art? Why do you think doctors are not enthusiastic about medicare? The pro is a businessman who deserves your support. Sure you can get things cheaper at Kresges, but what the hell—remember all the free advice you've wheedled out of him and the sympathy he has provided, without laughing, in your periods of travail. And remember how he lied

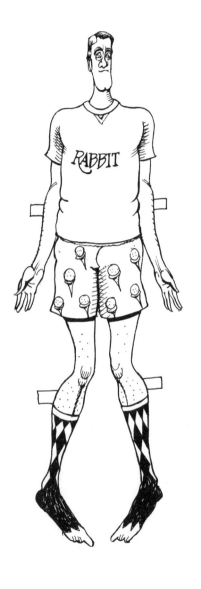

you are here …

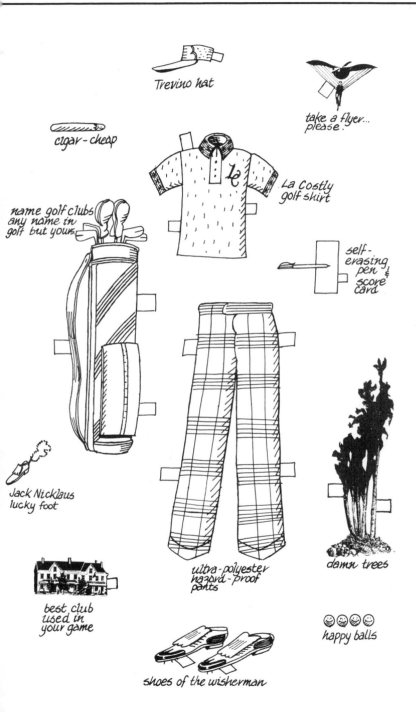

Trevino hat

take a flyer...
please.

cigar-cheap

La Costly
golf shirt

name golf clubs
any name in
golf but yours

self-
erasing
pen &
score
card

Jack Nicklaus
lucky foot

damn trees

best club
used in
your game

ultra-polyester
hazard-proof
pants

happy balls

shoes of the wisherman

for you that time when your wife phoned and you were out on your trap-line. Golf pros are nice people.

"I think I'll buy a new set of clubs," said Leo. "What do you think I should get?"

"Your head examined," said Doc.

"I don't think that would help," said Leo. "But there is so much conflicting information about various makes of clubs that I'm really in a quandary."

"You can thank the advertisers for that. You are an advertising agent yourself so you should know the score. Advertising is very useful in the business world because it induces people to buy things they don't want and can't afford, which enables those who make these things to buy stuff they don't want and can't afford. Advertising is therefore the backbone of the economy. And advertising agents are right at the bottom of that back-bone. Right there. Splut."

"Thank you," said Leo. "But I would appreciate your advice because I know you're a serious student of the game."

"Very well," said Doc. "The **First Law of Golf Clubs** (as promulgated by the pro) states: *the more expensive your clubs are, the better you will play.* This is undoubtedly true. If you don't think so, ask somebody who has recently put out a thousand clams for a new set of clubs with galvanated plutonium shafts and a gyroschitzik framistan in the head. He will rave about them—greater distance, greater accuracy, greater everything. Your suspicion that he is saying this because he doesn't want to admit that he was an idiot for buying them is unworthy of you."

"Oh, I wouldn't take that attitude," said Leo.

"You always play better with a new set of clubs—for awhile," said Doc. "It's a little like acquiring a new mistress. The freshness and newness are exciting until the novelty wears off, imperfections and limitations emerge, and you'd just as soon go back home—if the door isn't locked. Or, in our simile, if your old clubs are still available. Pride may intervene. The **Rule of Burning Bridges** (applicable to both the above situations) says: *never cast off the old until the new has proved satisfactory.*"

"I'll remember that," said Leo.

"The truth of the matter is that you can score just as well (I'm talking about clubs now) with four clubs as you would with a full set, *e.g.*, a wood, a putter and two irons. But if you don't want to be viewed with contempt by other afficionados you've got to go for the works."

"Okay," said Leo.

"Golf clubs are ill-designed for the purpose for which they are intended," said Doc. "If the objective of golf is to get a ball from position A to position B, there must be a better device. I don't know what it is, but there's got to be. Present clubs are obviously devised to make things difficult—the same mentality that came up with the idea of sand traps and water hazards."

"Why are clubs numbered the way they are?" asked Leo. "Are the numbers just for identification purposes, or is there some rationale involved?"

"There's a scientific basis for the numbering system," said Doc. "The **Rule of Club Numbers** states: *the higher the number of the club, the greater the potential for mischief.* For example: a three iron has a thirty per cent chance of things going awry; an eight iron has an eighty per cent chance, and so forth, right up to a pitching wedge, which is a ten iron and thus gives you a one hundred per cent chance of failure. A sand wedge is really an eleven iron, so you have a one hundred and ten per cent probability of lack of success. A recognition of this latter statistic gives you an appreciation of what to expect from this abominable club when you get into a sand trap."

"I've noticed," said Leo.

"I've noticed you noticing," said Doc.

"I've noticed you noticing my noticing," said Leo.

"The role of some clubs is self-explanatory," said Doc. "For example: a driver is for driving, a putter is for putting, and a wood is for long-distance shots into the woods. The role of irons is not quite so self-explanatory but, fundamentally, irons are for shanking. A **Refinement of the Rule of Club Numbers** states: *the higher the number of the club, the greater the possibility of shanking.* A shank is the most horrible shot in golf, in case you haven't noticed. There you are, preparing for a nice easy approach to the green. You can see in your mind's eye the ball flying nicely to the edge of the green with just enough force to run up to the hole. And what happens? The ball squirts off at a sixty degree angle into the trees. Disaster! Other golfers avert their eyes in sympathy and horror. Their principal concern, however, is that the condition might be contagious. Most golfers won't even say the word out loud because it might wedge in their subconscious; if they have to refer to the condition at all they spell it, and usually "chanque," to avoid contamination. But fortunately I am not superstitious; the fact that I carry a horseshoe in my pocket, always spit over my left shoulder and mutter a Druid invocation before every shot is irrelevant. The shanks, once they descend upon you, tend to linger. They may disappear for awhile and then, at the worst possible time, return to savage you again. While you are in the throes of the shanks, every iron shot is a nightmare. Efforts to eliminate shanks, such as changing your grip or your swing or your stance are counter-productive, in view of the **Refinement of the Refinement of the Rule of the Club Numbers** which states: *the apprehension arising from a previous shank increases the probability of another shank.* The answer, obviously, is not to be apprehensive. Ha!"

"Where on earth do you get all those rules and laws?" said Leo. "Are they published or listed somewhere?"

"No," said Doc. "They are fruits from the tree of knowledge which I have garnered during a wasted life of golfing frustration. We could formulate that into a law too, the **Law of Experience**: *the tree of knowledge bears only bitter fruit.*

"From that would arise a law of wisdom, would it not?"

"No. Knowledge does not necessarily lead to wisdom—particularly in golf."

"Well, you've talked a lot, but you haven't given me much advice on choosing a new set of clubs," said Leo.

"Now, that is wisdom," said Doc. "See the pro."

"While we are on the subject of clubs," said Leo, "what is that strange club I've seen you using when you come out of the trees left-handed?"

"A jigger. Also called a scrambler. A versatile and useful weapon for getting out of trouble."

"What's it like?"

"Here, I'll show it to you. It's a Janus club—two-faced, like your friends when they say 'tough luck'."

"I thought that club was illegal."

"No, it isn't," said Doc, "as long as you include both faces in your count of fourteen clubs. The jigger is the greatest thing since the discovery of the condom."

Preparations

There are a number of ways the duffer can prepare himself for his periodic onslaught upon the course. These include reading, practising, and lessons.

We can dispose of reading rather quickly. There is a plethora of books available on ways to improve your golf game. These texts are written by pros, each of whom rediscovers the wheel and puts a new hub-cap on it. Everything these books say is true, even when they contradict each other, but none of them will do anything for your game—I know because I've tried them all. Such books should be read for their cultural value, not instruction.

There is a substantial library on how to win without improving your game. These books are much more useful and I recommend them to you if you are a scoundrelly golfer (a redundancy?). I shall not take time here to discuss these books, but in essence they deal with ways to steer Murphy in the direction of your opponents. They are also useful to alert you to skulduggery when it is applied to you by others.

Everyone tells duffers that they should spend a lot of time on the practice fairway. The principal motivation for this advice is to get the duffers the hell off the course and leave it to real golfers. The practising duffer usually ingrains his bad habits and runs into the **First Law of Practice**: *the repetition of an error does not correct it.* On the other hand, the golfer may confuse himself by trying something different on every shot, and thereby discover the **Second Law of Practice**: *what works once won't work a second time.*

One thing you have to remember with regard to practice fairways is the **Paradox of Disparate Equals**: *things that are equal to the same thing are not necessarily equal to each other.* **Explanation**: *the yard markers on the practice fairway are closer to the tee than the same distance on the course.*

In order to avoid the unproductivity of self-tutelage, the only thing to do is to take some lessons from the pro. This won't work either. No fault accrues to the pro because everything he tells you will be one hundred per cent right—for him. You've got to remember that the pro has a completely different set of muscles than you do. He will show you how to hit the ball. Smooth, powerful, beautiful. You do exactly the same thing and zilch.

The teaching of golf uses the heuristic method, which is a system of education under which the pupil is trained to find out things for himself. The principal thing you find out is what doesn't work— and that's just about everything.

The primary problem with a lesson from the pro is that he will want to change the spastic twitch you call a swing into something smooth and functional. He will try to make you over into a facsimile of himself, ignoring all the adjustments you have introduced to allow for your slice, your dominant right eye, your flat feet, your gimpy knee, your sway, your ass sag, and your arthritis. The pro's job is a little bit like trying to straighten out a pretzel.

As a result of these factors you will soon discover the **First Law of Lessons**: *one lesson will screw up your game for a week; two lessons for two weeks, and so on.* In other words, it will take you that long to get back to playing only as badly as you did to start with.

The **Second Law of Lessons** states: *a lesson from the pro is like getting a loan from the bank—if you already have lots of money you get the loan; if you play golf well to start with, he can help you—if you don't, he can't.*

Let us now follow Leo out to the practice fairway for his first lesson from the pro and observe at first hand some of the problems of golfing pedagogy.

"Now, Mr. Bloom, I gather from what you say that your game is going pretty well but you feel that there are a few things not quite right. Very well. To start with would you just take a full practice swing so I can have a look at it.

"Hmm. Is that really your normal swing? It is? Do you always end up standing on your right leg with your left foot up in the air? You do. To give you power, you say. Well, that may be one of the little things that needs correcting. It is usually considered desirable to keep both feet on the ground. Palmer does, you know, and he has quite a bit of power. Now try another swing, keeping both feet on the ground.

"Oh, too bad. You hit your left foot with the club. Does it hurt? I'm sure it does. I see. So that's why you lift your left foot. Good thinking. However, maybe you should just open your stance a little. It's not really a good idea to have the left foot directly in front of the ball, you know. Try it again with an open stance.

"Much better. At least you didn't hit your foot that time. Now we'll throw down a ball and try hitting it with a five iron.

"You missed the ball completely because you didn't keep your head down. Take another shot keeping your head down.

"That's one of the biggest divots I've seen in a long time. It shows what tremendous power you have. All we need to do is harness it a bit. No, no, just leave the divot there. Don't try to lift it or you'll strain your back. I'll have one of my boys come over later with a machine to replace it. Now let's try it again. Someplace in between the last two shots—not a foot above and not a foot under it. What we want is a happy medium.

"Now that's what's known as an open-faced shank. Oops, it's heading over for the next fairway where those two ugly broads are standing. Fore! Whew! It missed them but that was close. By the looks of them it wouldn't have been much loss if you had hit them. One of them is waving.

"Oh, your wife, eh. The dark one who looks like a Spanish senorita? She's beautiful. When I said ugly, I meant the other one. Oh, your sister, eh? Well, win a few, lose a few.

"Who's that man your wife is playing around with? I mean a round of golf, of course. Oh, it's Hugh Boylan. Nice guy. Got quite a way with the ladies, I hear. But not to worry. Shall we get back to the lesson. Could I have your attention, Mr. Bloom? Mr. Bloom. Mr. Bloom! Stop looking over at the other fairway. Look at the ball. Now try it again.

"Much better. It was straight down the fairway, although with your great power you should be able to get more than ten yards. What you need is a big shift.

"I'm not being vulgar. I said shift. Shift. There's an 'f' in it. What I'm referring to is this: on your back swing you should transfer your weight to your right side, then on the swing you throw all your weight forward. Like this. See? Now try it.

"Well, you certainly threw your weight forward. But you forgot to hit the ball. My little joke. Here, let me help you up. Did you hurt yourself? No? Good. Now have another go at it, with not quite so much abandon. You must be under control at all times. Keep your head still, your right elbow in and your left arm straight. That's all there is to it.

"You didn't do any of those things but you did hit the ball. Amazing. We're making great progress. You haven't quite got the hang of transferring your weight from right to left. You've got to tighten up your poo muscle. As the fly said when he walked across the mirror, 'that's one way to look at it.' What it boils down to in vulgar terms is this: you've got to get your ass into the swing. And I might say, Mr. Bloom, in this respect you have a great deal to offer. My little joke. Ha, ha. Oh well.

"You have the ball a little too far back. Try hitting the ball off your left toe.

"It won't stay on your shoe? No. No. I didn't mean that. The ball is on the ground but opposite your left foot. Harry Vardon give me strength.

"That's better. If you hadn't looped on your back swing you might have hit it. I think you're a little tense, Mr. Bloom. Relax. And stop looking over at that other fairway. Your wife and Mr. Boylan have disappeared. Now you're gripping the club as if it were a rattlesnake that's going to bite you. You should grip the club gently, like you were holding a little bird that you didn't want to escape.

"Well, you got pretty good distance with your

club I must say. It went farther than the ball did last time. You have to hold it a little more firmly than that. I'll go and fetch it for you.

"Let me examine your grip. No, both hands are not supposed to be under the club. That's okay for baseball or hockey or dealing off the bottom of the deck, but not for golf. Oh, Doc Lynch showed you how to hold the club. He's quite a joker, isn't he. No, the hands should be on top, like this, with the fingers overlapping. So. Yes, it does feel awkward at first. Now try a swing.

"Oh, too bad. You hit your left foot again. We're back where we started. Remember to use an open stance. Another thing, are you flexing your knees? You're supposed to squat slightly. I can't tell because your pants are baggy at the back. Are you squatting, or is it just your pants that are squatting? You are. Good.

"I think we'll give some time now to trying to get you to hold your head still. You're moving your head a good two feet on your back swing. What I'll do is stand in front of you with my hand on your forehead while you swing under my arm. Like this. See? Good. Now swing.

"Oh, sorry. I didn't mean to stick my finger up your nose. Does it hurt? I suppose it does—nearly broke my finger. However, this exercise did demonstrate to you how much you are jerking your head about. Blow your nose and we'll try it again. Now remember, keep your head still. I'll hold my hand on your head and you swing under my arm.

Okay? Fine. Now swing.

"KEERIST! You hit me on the shin. Ooooo. You've broken my leg. Oooo. I'll never walk again. Great balls of fire. Let me sit down for a few minutes. Oh, my leg.

"There, the pain has let up a little. I'll tell you what I think, Mr. Bloom. I'll be perfectly honest with you. You have a tremendously powerful, unique, natural swing. I've never seen anything like it in thirty years of teaching. I'm afraid to suggest modifying it or I might spoil it. I'd suggest you go back to your old swing and just forget everything I told you. And I'll just limp over to the bar, put my leg up and have a big smash of scotch. Keerist. My leg. Good luck and goodbye, Mr. Bloom."

Retroactive Adjustments

There are various methods used by golfers to modify the flight of a ball after it has been hit. These manoeuvres are called "retroactive adjustments" or "post-shot corrections."

The principal procedure used is to shout instructions at the ball, such as, "go, go," "bite," "don't go there," "pull," "go left," "come around," or finally, in desperation, "hit something—a tree, a rock, my wife—anything."

Hugh was a particularly vehement exponent of this sort of thing. After one episode of unusual vociferousness, Doc said to him, "Hugh, I should point out to you that the **First Law of Retroactive Adjustments** states: *instructions shouted at a ball have the opposite effect to that requested.*"

"Did you see what that ball did? It didn't go where I hit it," shouted Hugh.

"That frequently happens," said Doc. "Balls have minds of their own. But could I caution you against your extensive use of body English. Such contortions put a severe strain on the spinal column, which undoubtedly accounts for the high incidence of the disc syndrome found in golfers. The term 'English' as applied to the curving of the path of a moving ball derives from billiards and was first used by Americans, who attributed a deviousness to that ilk which they have not had reason to modify. However, the **Second Law of Retroactive Adjustments** dictates: *body English applied to the flight of a ball has a positively negative effect.* Arms and legs waved at a ball have the same utility. Therefore, the combination of expostulation, body English and arm and leg flailing provides a synergistic reverse effect."

"How would you like to take a big flying jump in the lake?" said Hugh.

"Temper," said Doc. "I was just trying to be helpful."

"Your kind of help I can do without." Hugh stamped off down the fairway. Doc smiled quietly to himself. His ears had a pointy look to them.

Requests for advice, such as an impassioned, "What am I doing wrong?" should be considered as rhetorical questions not requiring an answer. It is an unwary golfer who gets his finger in that woodpecker's nest. If you do respond you will initiate an interminable dialogue which will screw up your own game. Furthermore, you will get the blame for every bad shot made later for giving bad advice. However, if you are a devious golfer, like Doc, then by all means respond, because of the **Law of Helpful Advice**: *there is nothing more unhelpful than helpful advice.*

Leo got a surprisingly good shot. "Hey," he cried in delight. "What did I do right?"

"I refuse to answer that," said Doc, "because it is unanswerable due to the **Law of Good Shots**, which states: *a good shot is the result of a series of compensating errors.* "

After a particularly bad shot, a golfer will frequently take a number of swings despite **Apodictic Law Number One**: *swings taken after a shot have no effect on the shot already made.* The golfer will go through a considerable series of analytical swings to determine what went wrong. The idea is that this analysis will correct the problem in the next effort. Not so. The **Corollary** to the preceding law states: *practice swings taken after a bad shot have no beneficial effect upon the next shot.* Sincere golfers will share generously with their colleagues a synopsis of their findings after every bad shot. Their associates cannot help but be impressed by the sagacity, sincerity, and graciousness of their friends. Some golfers will throw down a second ball and try the shot over again. This exercise is fatuous because, if the shot is good, he will curse himself for not doing it the first

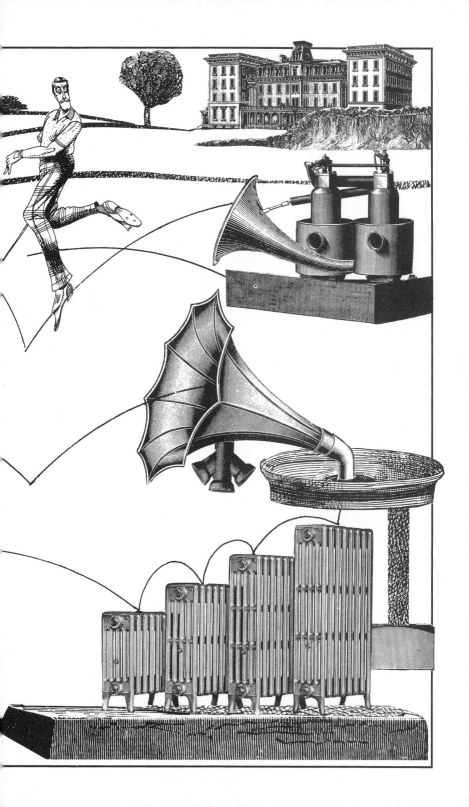

time; if the shot is bad, as it usually is, the disconcertion is compounded. Furthermore, the practice is illegal, dangerous, and immoral.

Exhortations are sometimes directed at putts. These entreaties usually take the form of a shouted "One time." The implication is that the ball has been unco-operative in the past and for once should go in—Murphy should not always prevail. Unfortunately, the instruction is usually left too late, to a time when it is quite apparent that the putt will not go in. Furthermore, the shout tends to startle the ball so that it jumps off line. The man making the putt will notice this but observers will not.

Instructions shouted at a ball tend to be profane. Swearing is as much a part of golf as hooks, slices, and grunches, and is frequently related thereto. Profanity on a golf course is, in reality, an invocation to Murphy.

Profanity can be an art form of considerable artistic merit. Unfortunately, profanity as employed in golf is usually a recapitulation of a few tried and true words and phrases which thereby lose their impact. But, in the hands of a gifted exponent, the genre can be a vehicle for inspired flights of fancy. Profanity derives from scatology, fornicology, and theology. The words should not be taken literally but regarded only as a vehicle for conveying deeply-felt emotions—the same role which a Stradivarius plays in the presentation of a Beethoven concerto. Doc does not swear routinely on the course, but when tried beyond human endurance he can interweave themes from the three basics into a contrapuntal fugue of inspired invective. At such times his associates stand in awe and reverence as the rich phrases roll out across the course. Great profanity cannot be delivered *sotto voce* but must be presented *fortissimo*. Sometimes his orations reach all the way to the next fairway or beyond.

"I believe in the therapeutic utility of profanity," said Doc. "Swearing relieves pressures, alleviates frustrations, and ameliorates tensions. If you keep things bottled up you will get ulcers, heart attacks, and purple flatulence. The only possible advantage to such pressure build-up is that you will blow the wax out of your ears. Profanity is a safety valve preferable to other means of emotional release such as: throwing your clubs—dangerous; wrapping your club around a tree—expensive; tossing your bag into the lake—awkward to recover; pounding the ground with your club—you may break your club; or stamping your foot—you may shatter an ankle. Profanity is good for you, but may cost you strokes because golf balls are delicate things which are offended by profanity, as witness the **Law of Sensitive Balls**: *a ball which has misbehaved on one shot and been sworn at will misbehave even more so on the next shot.*"

One topic related to profanity, because the vocabularies overlap, has to do with the risqué stories which are prevalent on golf courses. Most of the stories related to golf have been around since the first Scot shanked into Loch Ness and said "Goodness gracious." The phrase suffers in translation. There are few new golfing stories, but that doesn't mean that the old ones can't be repeated over and over again. Whenever a new story does emerge, or a fresh version of an old one is formulated, it is promptly carried around the world from Carnoustie to Mililani by peregrinating golfers. When golfers run out of golfing tales, as they do very quickly, they resort to stories of a more general nature, although, truth to tell, story-telling is usually a cloak for a feeble wit. Exponents of the genre therefore demonstrate the **Paradox of Story Telling**: *those least able to excel as raconteurs are those most insistent on telling stories.*

One gimmick to be on the watch for is the opponent who starts a story while you are getting ready to shoot and then says, "I'll tell you the punch line after you've hit." He wants you to be thinking about that punch line during your backswing when you should be concentrating on your shot. Make him finish the story.

The most effective method of retroactive adjustment has to do with the score card. A forgotten stroke is as good as a 250-yard drive. Since most adults can count to ten (ten fingers, you know), it is surprising how much difficulty golfers have in keeping track of figures up to that maximum. The simplest way to lose a stroke, while appearing to be frightfully conscientious, is to count backwards. Your opponent will say, "I took two putts, one out of the trap, one out of the rough and my drive. Yes, five." The fact that he was in the rough twice has been inadvertently forgotten.

"The **First Law of Golfing Accountancy**," said Doc, "states: *a mistake in scoring is seldom detrimental to the person making it.* From this basic principle a number of ancillary laws arise. The **Second Law of Golfing Accountancy** is: *your opponent has difficulty remembering all of his strokes; you have difficulty forgetting all of yours.*"

"An **Advisory Law** related thereto," said Stephen, "would read: *when in doubt about your own score, ask your partner, never your opponent.*"

"A valid bit of advice," said Doc. "I shall add to that by enunciating the **Law of Choice**: *if your opponent is in doubt about which of two figures represents the number of strokes he took on a particular hole, he will choose the smaller figure.*"

"The **Corollary** to that theorem," said Stephen, "is: *so will you.*"

Deportment

Our four heroes were again held up on the four-teenth tee by the senior foursome ahead. Hugh spent the interval bemoaning his back luck on the thirteenth where he had again run afoul of Murphy.

"Spare us your threnody," said Stephen.

"If you're looking for sympathy," said Doc, "you'll find it in the dictionary—on the same page with syphilis."

"I'd give you my crying towel, Hugh," said Stephen, "but it's still wet from the third hole."

"The **First Rule of Deportment**," said Doc, "is: *neither a weeper nor a boaster be.*"

"You had back luck, partner," said Leo. "Now in my own case...."

"Since I had a good score on the last hole," said Doc, "it would be unseemly of me to draw attention to the remarkable level of competence which made it possible, nor to contrast it with the miserable performance you put on. One should not take undue delight in the disasters of one's opponents, nor the good fortune of one's own team. However, human nature being what it is, one is less upset by the difficulties of one's opponents than by the bad luck of oneself; one should endeavour to bring sympathy and compassion to the former and restraint and good humour to the latter.''

"I haven't seen any sign of either, so far," said Hugh.

"The **Law of Golfing Confabulation**," said Doc, "dictates that: *a golfer will not hold forth unduly on his own problems or accomplishments, and will listen a reasonable length of time while others are sounding off.*"

"Yes, but what's a reasonable length of time?" asked Hugh.

"You've just used it up," said Doc.

"With his own blather, you will note," said Stephen.

"While we continue to wait for that group of paleontological artifacts ahead of us to finish playing statues, I shall further enlighten you on some deep philosophical truths relative to deportment."

"The Lyceum should have it so good," said Stephen.

"The **First Tenet of Gentlemanly Behaviour**," said Doc, "is: *everyone is a gentleman when his game is going well.* There is a **Corollary** to this, which goes: *you really get to know a man when his game goes sour.*"

"True," said Stephen. "Golf is diabolically designed to engender frustration, exasperation, and despair, and thus bring out the best and the worst in a man."

"Golf is therefore a microcosm of life," said Doc, "for it embraces elation and misery, success and failure, pleasure and suffering. A man's performance on the course reflects his approach to life."

"It takes courage to play badly," said Leo.

"No one who has just had a bad hole admires the view or comments on the beauty of the weather," said Hugh.

"Everyone is self-centred, unscrupulous, and immoral," said Doc, "but each person also has virtues of kindliness, honesty, and goodness. Golf provides a crucible for the interaction of these contradictory impulses. So does life. What a person really amounts to, intrinsically, results from this conflict between virtue and peccability."

"True virtue is unobtainable," said Stephen. "Therefore, the only virtue is the pursuit of virtue."

"Nobody is what they pretend to be," said Doc. "Everyone presents a façade of some kind to the world. Golf is an effective mechanism to see behind that façade."

"A golfer will pursue virtue but is frequently disappointed in himself because, under pressure, he does not come up to his own expectations—but

certified
crying tow

good sport
mask

special iron—
the par-none

he won't thereby surprise his friends," said Stephen.

"I read somewhere," said Leo, "that the best truck drivers are those that are not intelligent, because they are not deflected from the job at hand by extraneous thoughts. Maybe the same applies to good golfers—at least in their back-swings."

"Are you suggesting that good golfers are dumb?" asked Hugh.

"Maybe it helps," said Leo.

"I don't think your thesis hangs together," said Stephen. "The proposition would run as follows: good truck drivers are dullards; dullards are good golfers; therefore bad golfers are intelligent. I regret to say, sir, that your syllogism is false and you are the living refutation of your hypothesis."

"Hang on to it though, Leo," said Doc. "If your theory is valid, then after the way you've played today, you've got to be a genius."

"Thank you," said Leo.

"Leo is a sport," said Hugh. "Genetically speaking."

"I always try to be a good sport," said Leo.

"Good sportsmanship is a much over-rated virtue," said Doc. "The **Law of Good Sportsmanship** dictates: *always be dishonest.* How can that be, you cry. Don't you? Well, don't you?"

"How can that be, I cry," said Hugh.

"Thank you," said Doc. "I thought you'd never ask. I shall elucidate. In the subscription to the sophism known by the quaint term of good sportsmanship, it is always necessary to hide your true feelings—which is dishonest. When your opponents are clobbering you, then you are expected to accept the situation with apparent good grace, although you are seething with fury inside. You put on your 'good sport' smile, which is a grimace bearing a striking resemblance to the *risus sardonicus* seen in strychnine poisoning. When things are going well for you, then you must pretend to a modesty which you don't feel at all. You may make a passing reference to good luck although you are well aware that the happy situation is due to your brilliant play rather than good luck. Your opponents have good luck, you have great skill. All pretence to modesty is false modesty and therefore dishonest. Indeed, if I might digress for a moment, I would point out that modesty is itself a dubious virtue. The only people who can afford to be modest are those with sufficient accomplishments to countenance the denigration of the attainments which they acquired by immodesty. The truly modest man is defeated before he starts. Arrogance, not modesty, provides the stimulus to excel and the resolution to undertake the travail necessary to bring victory about. Nicklaus can afford to be modest because he has the confidence in himself and the audacity to aspire to be the greatest. I shall summarize the situation in a **Modest Paradox**: *immodesty is necessary to provide an excellence to be modest about.*"

"I have modesty thrust upon me," said Stephen.

"So do I," said Hugh. "But I fight it."

"Don't we all," said Doc. "But a wise man does not permit the perversity of a small ball to distort his personality nor embitter his life."

"Nor permit temporary fortuity to engender insolence," said Stephen.

"Quite so," said Doc. "But let me return to my dissertation on good sportsmanship. Now, where was I? Ah, yes. As I have indicated, good sportsmanship demands that you dissemble. You must hide your elation at your successes or be accused of gloating; and you must conceal your bitterness at your disasters or be described as a poor loser. Nobody is a good loser. Some people hide it better, that's all. If your partner is playing like a donkey, you must pretend that it doesn't really matter, although you would like to kick his ass up to his shoulders. If you yourself are playing badly, then you must affect a humbleness you don't feel. However, you may be able to drop a gentle comment about how you carried your partner on the first five holes, so it is now his turn. One final word: recognizing that the pretence to good sportsmanship is a sham, it is charitable not to chip the façade presented by your opponents. Good manners, for the most part, is simply a matter of condoning humbug. That finishes the lesson, brethren."

"Hallelujah," said Hugh.

"I'm glad you ended with a favourable, if somewhat muted, comment about good manners," said Stephen.

"Oh, I'm all for good manners," said Doc." The

First Law of Relationship with Your Opponent is: *always treat the bastard with great courtesy.* There is nothing more annoying than elaborate courtesy."

"How about your partner?" asked Leo.

"The **First Law of Relationship with Your Partner** is: *always treat the bastard with great courtesy,*" said Doc.

The Administration

Every club has an organizational structure to take care of its management. Details vary from club to club but the results are always the same, viz., dissatisfaction of the membership and exasperation of the administration.

The administration comprises two groups: the elected officials, who are chosen for reasons irrelevant to the job; and the civil service of experts to do the work. This dichotomy of authority allows ample opportunity for buck-passing—which, as I have indicated, always ends up with Murphy. The principal function of the experts is to take the blame when things go awry. The elected officers take the credit when things go right. A plethora of committees keeps the worms in the can in constant turmoil.

"What I don't understand," said Hugh, "is why anybody in his right mind would want to get elected to a committee and take all the flak they get."

"Who says they're in their right minds," said Stephen.

"Prestige," said Leo.

"An officer in this club has about the same level of prestige as a honey-wagon driver in Montana," said Doc.

"Some people enjoy the little brief authority to push other people around," said Stephen. "But everybody becomes a porcupine when they're pushed."

"Some very high-powered executives take on relatively minor offices," said Leo.

"And do a lousy job," said Hugh.

"Of course," said Stephen. "Because they don't know what they're doing. Look at George Spindlebog, he's president of an investment house, so they made him chairman of the greens committee. He thinks a ball-washer is a bidet."

"An executive is someone who carries his frisbee in a briefcase," said Doc.

"Doc," said Hugh, "you were on the Board for awhile, weren't you?"

"Yes, but I resigned when I got no support for my recommendation to make the showers co-educational. From the point of view of the Board, the **First Tenet of Administration** is: *when dealing with fools, there's no such thing as a fool-proof arrangement.*"

"I'll be the advocate for the other side," said Stephen, "and give you the **Second Tenet of Administration**: *if there's something stupid the Board hasn't thought of yet, they'll think of it.*"

"I don't know why we have so many committees," said Leo.

"The three objectives of a committee are: firstly, to keep the women off their backs; secondly, to keep the men quiescent; and thirdly, to make money. They invariably fail in all three," said Doc.

"The most formidable group in this club," said Hugh, "is the women's bridge club. Stir up a vipers' nest with your little finger if you want to, but leave that bridge group alone."

"I don't mind them playing bridge if they'd keep the hell off the course," said Doc.

"Women golfers are a fact of life you might as well accept," said Stephen. "Furthermore, the calumny heaped on women golfers is a base canard. The **First Paradox of Chivalry** is: *women are more gentlemanly on a golf course than are men.* They play faster than men. They don't knock the ball far, but they walk up and hit it bop, bop, bop, along the fairway, without the interminable cogitations peculiar to males. They don't hold seances on the green. They seldom get into trouble and if they do they throw the ball out."

"Women don't indulge in ratiocinations because they are ill-equipped to do so," said Doc.

"Nonsense," said Stephen. "Wouldn't you concede that Dorothy is highly intelligent?"

"Of course," said Doc. "She married me, didn't she?"

"Everyone is entitled to one mistake," said Stephen.

"Women get the fidgets when there're men playing behind them," said Leo.

"No wonder," said Stephen." The **Second Paradox of Chivalry** states: *women will invite men to play through; men never invite women to play through.*"

"Women golfers are the living refutation of Women's Lib," said Doc. "They're out on the course all the time, while hubby is getting duodenal ulcers down at the office. Why drive a combine when you can drive a golf cart?"

"There's too many of them," said Hugh.

"Women live longer than men. They do it on purpose," said Doc.

All clubs have a handicapping system; most have now gone to computers for the very good reason that you can't argue with a computer. The objective of a handicapping system is to enable players of diverse abilities to have a jolly, competitive game. It doesn't work that way at all. If the low handicapper beats the duffer, no credit accrues; if the tyro beats the expert, he is accused of having too high a handicap. For the most part, golfers very wisely play with those having similar handicaps.

Nobody plays anywhere near his handicap. Ask a golfer what his handicap is and he will hem and haw and then, if pressed, give you a figure but always add, "That's what it says on the board downstairs but I'm not playing anything like that well. I'm waiting for the computer to catch up." Anyhow, nobody is supposed to play consistently to his handicap. Low handicappers play closer to their handicaps than do duffers. A duffer may have a swing of fifteen strokes from day to day, which provides a variety and excitement not experienced by the experts.

"Golf is a competitive game," said Doc. "For glory or for money. Handicaps play a vital role in any contest. That's where you face the **First Law of Handicapping**: *your handicap is too low; your opponent's is too high.* This accounts for the tangled negotiations that go on before every match which result in the stroke situation staying exactly where it was to start with."

"It's very difficult to get extra strokes, I've observed," said Leo, "no matter how badly you're playing."

"Despite the law I have just promulgated," said Doc, "every golfer tries to play well and thereby lower his handicap. This is a paradox because of the **Second Law of Handicaps** which reads: *the lower the handicap, the less fun a golfer gets out of golf.* The expert expects to have a good round and is devastated when he doesn't; the rabbit expects to have a lousy round and is delighted when he doesn't. A duffer breaking a hundred is happier than an expert breaking par."

"Yet every golfer is a pro manqué," said Stephen.

"I'm happy when I break a hundred," said Leo.

"The very low handicappers are the biggest snobs in the club," said Doc. "You hear them in the bar complaining loudly about blowing to five over par. Piffle. This raises the **First Law of Phoning**, which is: *a low handicapper never phones a duffer for a game.* A **Corollary** to that law is: *a high handicapper, if he has any sense at all, never phones a low handicapper.* If he does, the elusive toe-dancing is a wonder to behold."

"It's interesting," said Stephen, "that at club meetings, the low handicappers try to have the course made more difficult—more traps, more water holes, contour mowing and so forth—whereas the rest of us want the course made easier. As a result, the course stays exactly as it was."

"I think the course is adequately difficult now," said Leo.

Chicanery is not unknown in handicapping. Some people just don't turn in their low scores and anyone who wins consistently is accused of this practice whether or not it is true. Certainly, as Calcutta time approaches, the entry of low scores falls off dramatically. In my own experience, it is hard to get away with such perfidy. If, by the grace of Murphy, I happen to get a low score, I find that my friends keep an eagle eye on the record book to make sure it gets entered. They will even be so helpful as to record it themselves if I happen to forget.

On the other hand, some golfers enter their low scores but not their high scores to maintain a low handicap for prestige purposes. Then when they play their usual game they can complain bitterly that they are having a bad round. This is a harmless practice which is benignly condoned by opponents as they rake in the pigeon's money. What price prestige?

"I have a theory," said Doc, "that the optimum handicap for happiness is sixteen. Below that figure you start to take the game too seriously; above it you are increasingly an exasperation to yourself and a trial to your friends. There is a good deal of evidence in support of the premise that the objective of golf is not fun but something else—I'm not sure what. But if you subscribe to that philosophy, good luck, go ahead, become a scratch golfer, but remember that the better you get, the more isolated you become. As we have observed, experts only want to play with experts and average golfers don't want to play with them. There are many more rabbits than there are tigers, so a duffer has a much greater number of potential partners from which to choose. I shall summarize the situation in the **Third Law of Handicaps**: *the lower your handicap, the fewer people will want to play with you.*"

"The rationalization of a dub," said Stephen.

"Of course," said Doc.

"Why does the Board insist on sponsoring so many tournaments," said Leo, "and scheduling them on weekends? They're a big nuisance."

"The objective is to break up the cliques, who bitterly resent this intrusion upon their well-established rituals. The Board, in its wisdom, fosters the idea that promoting such tournaments will enable members to get to know each other by playing together. This certainly works. Undying enmities are frequently engendered in this way."

"Tournaments are okay for the women," said Hugh, "but they ought to leave the men alone. Tournaments always screw up the regular matches."

"That brings to mind," said Doc, "the ultimate golfing monstrosity—mixed two-ball tournaments. Mixed two-ball matches have ruined more marriages than adultery."

"Molly won't play with me in mixed two-balls," said Leo.

"Tournaments usually involve draws, which are subject to certain laws," said Doc. "The **First Law of the Draw** is: *if there is someone in the club you particularly detest, you will be drawn against him.*"

"An **Adjunct** to that law," said Stephen, "is: *he will beat you.*"

"Shades of Garfinkle," said Hugh.

"With regard to women's tournaments," said

Doc, "there is a **Second Law of the Draw**, which states: *your wife and your mistress will be drawn against each other.* And there is a **Corollary** to that law: *whoever wins, you will be the loser.*"

The Home Front

There are probably a number of reasons why an amiable relationship on the home front is desirable, but the most important one is to provide a basis for good golf. You can't play a good round if you have just had a fight with your wife or are anticipating one on your return, or, as is more likely, both.

The criterion for determining how things stand around home is based on your Brownie Point balance. You get Brownie Points when you do things which please your wife and lose them when you do otherwise. A golfer has to pay a great deal of attention to his Brownie Point accumulation. A non-golfer has a much easier time of it unless he has another hobby, such as running a trap-line.

The basic problem for golfing husbands arises from Mrs. Murphy's Law—husbands just have a talent, it seems, for screwing things up even with the best intentions. Hubby can arrive home reasonably early thinking everything is hunky-dory only to find that he is getting the "Silent Treatment" for something or other. This manifestation of wifely displeasure may trigger hubby's recollection to the fact that today was the day Jon and Phyllis were coming over for a back-yard bar-b-q and he was supposed to pick up the steaks and charcoal and be home early to get the whole show on the road. Oh boy! Brownie Points down the tube.

"The **First Law of Brownie Points**," said Doc, "is: *there's more ways to lose Brownie Points than to gain them.*"

"Tell us O Master," said Stephen, "what are the ways one can accumulate Brownie Points? Let us bathe in the font of your knowledge, O Wise One. And perchance, sir, you will be so kind as to continue your accustomed procedure of formulating your observations in Hammurabian tenets."

"I don't think the Babylonians played golf," said Leo.

"Very well," said Doc. "I shall accept your challenge, although you confuse impertinence with wit, sir. Any activity which finds favour in your wife's eyes is a plus, no matter how trivial or ridiculous—such as cutting the lawn, weeding the garden, washing the windows, or painting the fence. When you return from a round of golf you should listen to her recounting of what transpired around home during your absence and pretend an interest. Give up a round once in awhile, drawing attention thereto, for important family affairs, like Aunt Sarah's birthday party. Spend a weekend at the lake with the family occasionally during the summer. Get home in time to take her to the opera—you can tee off early that day. Take her out to dinner once in a while and to some place other than the club. Offer to take a turn driving little Cedric to his classical ukulele lessons. The **Second Law of Brownie Points** is: *always try to maintain a credit balance.* It is easier to keep up than to catch up. Some words of warning: if you've had a bad round, don't come home and kick the dog—he may bite you. So may your wife.''

''Wives don't seem to be very interested in your golf,'' said Leo.

''Sure they are,'' said Doc. ''Surprisingly enough, however, giving your wife a blow-by-blow account of your round doesn't gain you any Brownie Points, and indeed may lose you some under the heading 'All you ever think about is golf.' However, marriage is for sharing, even if vicariously, so you owe it to your wife to keep her informed of your activities on the course. She may pretend that she isn't interested but she is, really, deep down. That glazed look and pretense of inattention is assumed. So don't be disconcerted if your account doesn't elicit the admiration or sympathy you might expect. Persevere.''

''It helps if your wife is a golfer,'' said Leo.

''Of course,'' said Doc. ''Women aren't much

given to detailed recapitulations, which is much to their credit, but if she does embark upon an account of her round, you should feign an enthusiasm and for Pete's sake don't interrupt, even if you yourself haven't finished a sentence around home in the last twenty years. The advantage of permitting her to complete her story is that she can scarcely complain then when you get on to more important matters—namely your own performance.''

"Successful marriages are built on reticence, chicanery, and deviousness," said Stephen.

"And love," said Leo.

"That too," said Stephen.

"If your wife is a golfer," said Doc, "you should waste a round once a week by joining her in the Powder Puff League, even if it means playing thirty-six holes that day."

"In my experience," said Stephen, "when playing with one's wife it is unwise to offer advice, even when asked. You can blow your Brownie Points forthwith if you fall into that trap. Also you shouldn't be careless and ask her advice on your game or she will probably give it to you. Women don't understand rhetorical questions."

"True," said Doc. "Now some further laws concerning Brownie Points. The **First Law of Sacrifice** reads: *a sacrifice that interferes with your golf gains more Brownie Points than one which is not related to golf.* For example, if you give up watching a football game on TV to go to a PTA meeting, it doesn't help much on your golfing Brownie Points. Your wife has a separate page in her mental ledger for golf. A **Corollary** to the above law states: *sacrifices made when the weather is too lousy for golf don't count.* If you are deep in the red, heroic measures are called for—buy her a fur coat or a new car. However, you must recognize that this credit will be dissipated surprisingly rapidly and you'll soon be back to a zero again."

"Gee," said Leo. "If I bought Molly a car I think I'd be in her good books for a long time."

"Not as far as golfing Brownie Points are concerned," said Doc. "It is better to maintain a small credit balance than to try to establish a large credit which you anticipate will last a long time. Look at our friend Murray. He took his whole family to Hawaii and, by arrangement, *didn't play golf.* What heroism! What a sacrifice! He thought the Brownie Points obtained in this way would last him all summer. On his return, this credit was shot in a week and he was back accumulating minor points the hard way."

"It doesn't seem fair," said Leo.

"Credits and debits in Brownie Point accounting don't work like they do in a bank," said Doc. "The **First Paradox of Brownie Point Accounting** is: *a credit balance doesn't earn interest, but is quickly depleted by service charges; a debit balance increases by compound interest.* Therefore most golfers continually operate from a deficit position."

"I've noticed that," said Leo.

"All this is a noetic exercise, as far as Hugh is concerned," said Stephen. "He's a bachelor—more or less. Historically, the term 'bachelor' referred to a young knight serving under another man's banner. How apt."

"I golf when I want to," said Hugh.

"You're missing a lot," said Leo.

"So I gather," said Hugh.

"The matter of children in a golfer's home presents a thorny problem," said Doc. "If you get the gears about being away so much playing golf that you don't know your own children, then you must take careful steps to refute the allegation. Make a list of your children's names and memorize it. If you want to go all out, put down their ages, school grades and other pertinent information, such as that Bernice is taking ballet lessons and Cedric is a homosexual. To avoid the embarrassment of mistaking one of the neighbour's kids for one of your own, a good idea is to obtain pictures of your children to be attached to their files. You can get pictures from your wife on the pretence of sentimental attachment. It might be a politic action to request a picture of your wife too, although you are not apt to forget what she looks like unless you are a very avid golfer. You should update from time to time so that you don't make the mistake of asking Cedric how things are going in Grade seven when it turns out he is in second year Pre-Med."

"I think you're exaggerating slightly," said Leo.

"The ways of losing Brownie Points are myriad and embrace anything related to golf which disrupts your wife's concept of home affairs. The principal no-no is being late for dinner, or not coming home at all. You can deplete a large credit balance at one fell swoop by arriving home at midnight boiled as a billy-goat after celebrating the first time you ever broke ninety. Wives don't understand these things."

"One thing I've learned," said Stephen, "is to keep my golfing treasures in my locker. My wife gave my hand-forged Forgan putter to her brother because she said it was obviously old and all worn out and he was just starting to play so it would be good enough for him. It cost me a fortune to get it back from him and lost me some Brownie Points to boot."

"That's nothing," said Doc. "My wife gave my favourite sweater to the Thrift Shop. I got it at Carnoustie twenty-three years ago and wore it when I won the fifth flight of the East Pidlington Open. I loved that sweater."

"Another thing I've learned," said Stephen, "is never tell your wife how much you lost or won. The former will elicit comments about dental bills and the overdraft at the bank; the latter will get sugarplums dancing in her head about a new mink stole, or some other ridiculous meretricious frippery."

"Have you ever noticed," said Doc, "that most golfers have pet names for their wives which they only use on the course. If you ask a guy if he can play next Thursday, he'll say 'I think so but I'll have to check with The Boss,' or some such term. These names usually imply a superior authority such as: The General, The Chairman of the Board, The Sergeant-Major, or The Speaker of the House. Other names are more ambiguous, such as: My Welterweight, Old Snarly, The Ball and Chain, The Tiger, The Voice, or The Oracle. There is some hazard to this, because when you introduce your wife to a colleague he may blurt out, 'I always wanted to meet Fred's Old Snarly, I've heard so much about you.' This is more apt to happen with bachelors—husbands have more sense.''

''We've had fun maligning our wives,'' said Stephen, ''so let me take a page from the files of the Old Master and be the angel's advocate by presenting some golfing laws from the point of view of the distaff side. The **First Law of Distaff Assessment**: *the lower the husband's handicap, the more weeds in the backyard.* The **Second Law**: *a rain which is too heavy for cutting the lawn in is just right for golf.* The **First Law of Selective Recall**: *a husband who can't remember whether he is to get a loaf of bread or a quart of milk when he gets to the store, can tell me which club he used for his second shot on the fourteenth hole a week ago.* And finally, bless their hearts, the **Ultimate Law of Wifely Tolerance**: *I'd rather have him out on the course chasing a ball than somewhere else chasing a blonde.*''

The Nineteenth Hole

Ah, the nineteenth hole. The refuge from cares and woes; the panacea for broken dreams; the solace for fractured psyches; alibi haven; Murphy's temple.

We join our battered heroes as they trudge into the bar, carrying Leo upon his shield—figuratively speaking. They thread their way between the crowded tables from which arises a hubbub of exuberant voices raised in happy expostulation, argument, and plain garden variety sounding-off. The room has a pleasant ambience of alcoholic good-fellowship.

"Here comes the Irish foursome. Batten the hatches."

"Erin go bragh."

"The Scots are sots but the Erse are worse."

"Hi, Leo. Have a good round or did you play your usual game?"

"Not very good. You see my right arm...."

"Hey, Stephen, want to match cards?"

"No thanks, Bert. You're too eager. I've seen your putting thaumaturgy too often."

"You missed a chance. I was running a bluff. I shot a horrible eighty-seven."

"Tough titty. I should be so horrible."

"Hey, Doc, have you guys got a cure yet for golfers' elbow?"

"You haven't got golfers' elbow, you've got drinkers' elbow. I'll send you a bill in the morning."

"Up yours."

"Let me tell you what happened to me on the fourteenth. You wouldn't believe."

"I believe."

Our friends seat themselves with exaggerated weariness at a vacant table.

"Ah, the men's bar," says Doc, with a deep sigh, looking around the room. "The last refuge of the male chauvinists. I love it. I love the zest, its congeniality, its vulgarity. The nineteenth hole makes the whole day worth while." He stretches his legs in luxurious ease. From nearby tables snatches of conversation float by. Murphy's influence is much in evidence.

"At the end of five holes I was two under, then I three-putted two greens. Then I...."

"That's nothing. I four-putted the thirteenth after getting on in two. When the yips hit you...."

"I'm two up, I'm three up, I'm four up.... No I'm
not. You get a stroke there, you sandbagger. I'm
three up...."

"Where's Fred today?"

"He's working on his Brownie Points. He's been
in the dog-house around home ever since the last
stag poker party."

"If my ball hadn't caught that stupid branch on
the seventeenth...."

"If the dog hadn't stopped to have a crap, he'd
have caught the rabbit."

"I'm two up at the end of nine. Remember that.
I'm one down, I'm two down...."

"Hey, I made two bucks off of Harry. It ain't
much but it's better than a slap in the belly with a
mahi-mahi."

"Have you heard the one about the three chorus
girls and the bishop?"

"Consolidated Western was down three points
this morning and I bought fifty thousand yesterday.
Wouldn't you know it."

"The ultimate ignominy—I even lost seven bucks
to Angus."

"We got behind Horace and his group of spastics
today. They were so slow I thought rigor mortis had
set in."

"There's no use complaining. Criticism rolls off
them like butter off a dog's whack."

"Sid's putter was hotter than love in spring-time
today. Sank them from all over the place."

"One thing I can't stand is a smart-ass."

"How do you live with yourself?"

"I'm three down. I'm four down...."

"Everyone talks. No one listens," says Hugh.

"Listen some time as an experiment," says Doc, "and you'll understand why nobody listens."

"You hear nothing in the bar but stories of disasters," says Hugh. "Didn't anybody have a good round?"

"After a picnic you remember the mosquitoes but not the butterflies," says Doc.

"A golfer is only interested in his own game," says Leo, "so that's all he talks about. But nobody else is really interested."

"It all goes in one ear and out the other end," says Hugh.

"The **First Rule of the Golfing Bore**," says Doc, "is: *the insistence of a golfer to tell you about his dull and tedious triumphs and tribulations is directly proportional to his reluctance to listen to the exciting and amazing account of your own performance.*"

"Total recall is a vice," says Stephen, "peculiar to golfers."

"Where is that girl?" says Hugh. "I need a drink."

"Don't we all."

"How much do I owe?" asks Leo.

"Plenty," says Doc, "with all those presses your partner threw at us. So you won't be buying any drinks, thanks to the **Immutable Rule of the Chit**, which states: *the winners on the course buy the drinks.*"

"That rule leads to the **Law of Diminishing Returns**," says Stephen, "which is: *every dollar you win on the course costs you five in the bar.*"

"You've got the card, Hugh," says Doc. "Figure out who owes what to whom. The **Aphorism of the Old Philosopher** states: *the paying off of bets is enjoyed more by some than by others.* I wouldn't be asking if I didn't think I had joy in store. Do the team bets first and then the individual matches."

"I know I'll be paying Stephen a bundle," says Hugh. "If I'd sunk that last two-foot putt on the eighteenth I'd have won the Aloha press and re-couped. Two feet. And the ball was in and jumped out!"

"Revenge is sweeter than flowing honey," says Stephen.

"I forgot my wallet," says Leo.

"Then you'll have to write a cheque," says Doc. "The **Rule of Betting Pay-Offs** states: *all bets must be paid forthwith and in cash.* No chits, no IOU's, no postponements, no 'I'll pay laters.'"

"I didn't bring a cheque."

"Then you have three alternatives: phone Molly to come and bail you out, sign over your clubs, or slash your wrists."

"Molly wouldn't come."

"Didn't it occur to you that there was just a bare possibility you might lose, Leo?"

"Not really. At least I hoped not. You see I took a lesson and...."

"Aha. Hubris leads to nemesis. Slash your wrists."

Betting is an integral part of golf. The level of betting varies considerably depending on affluence, temerity, and pretentiousness. My own credo on gambling is a simple and flexible one, viz., the **Formula for Wagers**: *golf bets should be at a level sufficient to add piquancy to the game without undue strain on the losers nor unseemly joy to the winners.* If you play golf for the purpose of making money from your friends you're playing golf for the wrong reason.

Hustlers abound on golf courses but they're not golfers as I understand the term—they're businessmen. *Caveat emptor.* Never bet more than you can afford to lose, don't be hornswoggled into betting more than you want to, and beware of automatic escalating presses. It's a good idea to clarify where the decimal point is when making bets with strangers. For example, if the bet is stated as one, one and one, you may think you are playing for a buck and find later you are in for a hundred, which, with presses, can run into quite an untidy sum. There goes the old homestead!

There are certain apparent inconsistencies in betting practices. For example, the **First Paradox of Betting** discloses: *the more affluent the golfers, the lower the stakes.* For one thing, they don't need the money and, for another, they probably have a deep affection for the stuff. The well-to-do player will get more joy or cry more loudly over winning or losing a few bucks on the golf course than making or dropping a bundle on the stock market. The amount involved in the match is not an important factor. The big gamblers are those least able to afford it. Everyone can afford to win, but if a wager hurts someone, it isn't fun—for either the hurter or the hurtee.

In general, the wealthier the golfer, the higher the handicap, which leads to the **Second Paradox of Betting**: *the lower the handicap, the higher the stakes.* This comes under the heading of "Vanity Betting," and is a macho thing—the hotshots bet big. The two paradoxes are paradoxically complementary. The low handicapper got that way by spending a lot of time on the golf course, thereby neglecting business and is less affluent. The high handicapper is a poor golfer because he works hard and makes a lot of money; or he worked hard all his life to be financially able to take up golf at a time when he isn't able to play golf worth a darn. He's learned the value of a buck and isn't about to lose a week's wages on a missed putt. This attitude also explains the **Paradox of the Slow Reach**: *the more affluent the golfer, the slower the reach for the chit in the bar.* If you were born with a silver putter in your mouth, none of the paradoxes apply.

Two attractive waitresses converge upon the table of our four friends.

"After a long and hazardous voyage, we are

rescued," says Doc. "Bronze Lydia and Golden Mina, welcome my lovelies. What a plethora of pulchritude. What a nadir of cerebral evolution."

"Oh, Doctor, you say the nicest things," says Lydia. She giggles and bats her eyes at him. "Did youse play good today?"

"Only well enough to make money."

"That's good enough. What would you like, sir?"

"I know what I'd like but I'll settle for a drink."

"I know their bad habits," says Mina. "Will you have the usual all 'round, gentlemen—three Old Bushmills on the rocks and one orange float with a jigger of vodka. Correct?"

"How did you remember," says Hugh.

"How could I forget. Nobody else in the club drinks any of them things."

"A taste for Irish whiskey is a cultivated depravity," says Stephen.

"Three drinks and one pablum," says Doc.

"The ice-cream puts a protective coating over the mucosa," says Leo. "You see my stomach...."

"Spare us please," says Hugh.

"And repeat the order at ten minute intervals until we fall off our chairs," says Stephen.

"Okay," says Mina.

As Mina turns to leave, Leo runs his eye lingeringly up her thigh to her red panties.

"Don't drool, Leo," says Hugh.

"Window shopping doesn't cost," says Doc.

"He that committeth adultery in his mind hath sinned," says Stephen.

"Absolution please," says Hugh.

"Stay with your succubi, Leo," says Doc. "You'll frolic with a better class of companion than you could otherwise attract."

"I was just looking," says Leo. "Weren't you?"

"Of course."

"Sirens in panty-hose," says Stephen. "An anachronistic travesty."

"Pour wax in my ears," says Doc. "I can still hear the music. Though dimly."

"I think the young ladies enjoy being looked at," says Leo.

"Of course they do," says Doc. "And they know they're safe in here. This place is a geriatric kindergarten."

"All peek and no boo," says Hugh.

"I deeply regret my mis-spent youth," says Doc. "My regret is that I wish I had it to mis-spend all over again. I am sadly aware of the **First Axiom of Non-Renewable Resources**: *when nubile wenches start calling you 'sir,' you're over the hump.*"

"To turn our attention from the callipygian cuties to the other side of the groin," says Stephen, "I see the steatopygous set is in session." He points to a table in the corner where a group of men are playing cards in a cloud of cigar smoke.

"The ward of twitchy prostates," says Doc.

"Fortunes change hands every twenty minutes," says Hugh.

"Not bloody likely," says Doc. "Old Horace is as

tight as a duck's poo muscle, which, in case you don't know it, is very tight indeed—otherwise the duck would fill up with water and sink.''

"I thought the phrase was 'tight as a bull's arse','' says Stephen.

"Bulls don't go in swimming,'' says Leo.

Mina arrives with the drinks, which she places in front of them.

"That'll put starch in your dickie, sir,'' she whispers to Doc.

"Oh, you naughty girl,'' says Doc. "I love you. Bring me a gallon of the stuff and I'll meet you later in the parking lot.''

Mina giggles and walks away with an exaggerated sway of the hips, well aware that four pairs of appreciative eyes are following her.

Doc raises his glass and examines the amber fluid. "Ah,'' he says. "Usquebaugh. A poteen brew, distilled from the dew of shamrocks collected by the light of a full moon by an Irish virgin—a rare creature. Here's to us.''

The four men sip their drinks appreciatively.

"I drank my first Bushmills,'' says Doc, "many years ago, on the shores of the Liffey with Bella, an old bawd from the old sod. A wonderful evening. Sort of a Celtic barmitzvah.''

"Circe and her hand-maidens, Zoe, Flora and Kitty. I knew them well,'' says Stephen.

"So did I,'' says Leo.

"Did you now,'' says Hugh. "You're a dirty old man, Leo.''

"I wasn't always a bishop," says Leo.

"The **First Law of Happy Senescence**," says Doc, "is: *the dirty old men are the happiest old men, but you have to lay the ground-work early.*"

"And Leo is the paradigm of the **Peter-Out Principle**," says Stephen, *"roués rise to their level of impotence."*

"Well, gentlemen," says Doc, "are we going to do what we ought to do and go home or are we going to make a night of it? If I read the signs aright, Leo is afraid to go home, Stephen is feeling festive because he won today, Hugh is loosey-goosey as usual and my Brownie Points are in such disarray that another blot on my escutcheon will make no never mind. What do you say?"

"Agreed," says Stephen. "We'll have several more rounds of drinks and then play b.s. poker for the dinner."

"I always lose at b.s. poker," says Leo.

"I had that in mind," says Stephen.

"I'm amenable," says Hugh.

"Wonderful, wonderful, wonderful," says Doc, leaning back happily. "To quote somebody or other on the ultimate law of laws, the **Apotheosis of Golf**: *golf is not a game, golf is a way of life."*

Edited by John Newlove
Designed by David Shaw
Composed by Attic Typesetting
Printed and bound in Canada by
T. H. Best Printing Company Ltd.